Answers
to the
Cultist
at Your
Door

Robert &
Gretchen
Passantino
and
RAYMOND SCHAFER

HARVEST HOUSE PUBLISHERS
Eugene, Oregon 97402

Except where otherwise indicated, all Scripture quotations in this book are taken from The Holy Bible, New International Version, Copyright © 1978 by the New York International Bible Society. Used by permission.

Answers To The Cultist At Your Door

Copyright ©1981 by Harvest House Publishers
Eugene, Oregon 97402

Library of Congress Catalog Card Number 80-83850
ISBN 0-89081-275-6

Printed in the United States of America.

FOREWORD

It is with great pleasure that I recommend *Answers to the Cultist At Your Door.* Robert and Gretchen Passantino and Raymond Schafer provide solid, Biblical, workable answers that effectively bring the gospel of our Lord Jesus Christ to those who are lost in the world of the cults.

I first met Robert and Gretchen Passantino over eight years ago at one of my lectures on the cults. They were relatively new in the field, witnessing mostly to Jehovah's Witnesses, and they wanted to express to me their appreciation for the tutoring that my books on the cults had given them. I prayed for them that night, asking God's blessings on their earnest desires to help the lost. Today they are testimonies to what hard work, dedication, and God's leading can accomplish.

The Passantinos enjoyed a successful professional relationship with me as research associates at my Christian Research Institute for over five years. Through working and learning under me, we came to feel a warm personal bond. I was glad to be used of the Lord to help them join the team.

Raymond Schafer's practiced editorial pen has polished several of my books for the last five years. I appreciate his gifted and diverse skills in editing and writing.

When my ministry began, almost thirty years ago, I prayed for God to raise up other dedicated Christians to help fight the battle with me. Robert and Gretchen Passantino and Raymond Schafer are three of those whom the Lord has added to the ranks. When my textbook, *Kingdom of the Cults,* was written fifteen years ago, I prayed that other books would supplement its contents to bring the truth to as many people as possible. This book is helping to do that job.

Walter Martin
San Juan Capistrano
California

INTRODUCTION

Answers to the Cultist At Your Door is designed to arm you with the essentials of the gospel message in terms that are understandable to the cultists you meet. The principles in this book are easy to understand, easy to remember, and true to God's Word, the Bible. We begin with a brief discussion of why people join the cults and what they are taught. Then we present concise summaries of five of the fastest-growing cults in America, with solid answers to their claims and effective ways to reach them with the truth of Christianity. Our conclusion gives you step-by-step plans for keeping your loved ones out of the cults and for reaching those you love who are in the cults.

This book is not meant to be a college text on cultic phenomena, nor is it meant to be a reference book for professionals in cult ministries. We recognize the importance of exhaustive treatments of the individual cults: we have been in the field for over a decade, and our library contains almost every book ever written on the cults, as well as countless publications written by cultists.

However, we also recognize the need of the nonprofessional to have answers for the everyday challenges to his faith. It is possible to have workable answers for the Mormon missionary at your door without having to digest three thousand pages on Mormon history and earning a doctorate in theology. There are many more complicated and in-depth refutations to cultic doctrine that we could have used, and the interested reader is welcome to write to us for suggestions on studying particular areas exhaustively. However, in this book we chose to couple clear Bible passages with common sense in answering the cults. We are confident that, with these uncomplicated answers, anyone can answer the cultist at his door.

Robert and Gretchen Passantino
Raymond Schafer

CONTENTS

1/ WHY THE CULTS COME KNOCKING

Gail carefully peeked out the window to see who had just rung her doorbell. A middle-aged couple, man in a conservative suit and woman in a soft pastel dress, stood at the door, each holding a small magazine and a small green book. Jehovah's Witnesses!

Conflicting emotions rose in Gail, a young Christian housewife. She had just heard a lecture in her Sunday school class about the cults, and she knew that the Jehovah's Witnesses denied the Trinity and would rather die than take blood transfusions. In one way she was eager to talk with the couple, to share with them her newfound faith in Jesus as her personal Savior. On the other hand, she had always been shy about confronting people or even talking amicably with strangers.

Before she became a Christian she had ignored the Witnesses who came to her door, thinking them to be self-deluded religionists who used their faith as a crutch because they couldn't face the world. After she became a Christian she knew that there was something different about them, and that they didn't accept her evangelical church as Christian, but she still didn't want to talk with them. She felt vaguely guilty, as if she should witness to them just like she did to anybody else, but she just didn't know enough to face them. During the last year they had come only once while she had been at home, and then she had avoided talking with them by saying that she was in a hurry and didn't have time to talk.

But today was different. Her Sunday school teacher had explained very clearly the differences between what she believed and what the Witnesses believed. He had given the class Scriptures which they could use to show the Witnesses that the Trinity was Biblical and that Jesus was God. The teacher had even passed out some tracts written especially for Jehovah's Witnesses. Her indecision was resolved. Gail prayed quickly, picked up the tracts she still had in her Bible from Sunday school, and opened the door.

THE GOOD NEWS OF GOD'S LOVE?

"Good morning, ma'am. We're visiting homes in your neighborhood today, sharing with people the good news of God's love for them. I'm sure you'll agree that in today's world of crime, inflation, and war the assurance of God's love is very important for us all. Don't you agree?" The man waited for Gail's reply, appearing genuinely concerned with her answer.

Gail hadn't really expected that line from him. Her Sunday school teacher had said that Jehovah's Witnesses believed that God accepted them on the basis of their meritorious service to their organization, the Watchtower. She had thought they would be afraid of God. "Well, yes, I do think God's love is important. I'm a born-again Christian and I know that God loves me. He sent His Son to die for my sins, and yours too."

The woman interrupted, "Oh, yes, as God's Son, Jesus was a perfect sacrifice for our redemption. Because of His sacrifice we can have a life in harmony and peace with God. Our magazine, *The Awake,* talks about that sacrifice and what it can mean for us today. Would you like a copy of it?"

"But you're Jehovah's Witnesses, aren't you? You don't believe in the Trinity. How can you say that Jesus is God's Son but not believe that He is God?" Gail asked.

"Of course we believe that Jesus is God's Son. The Bible tells us in John 17:3 that everlasting life comes from believing in Jehovah, the only true God, and in Jesus Christ, His Son. I'm sure you would agree with that verse, since as a Christian you believe in the Bible. Now if the Bible itself tells us that there is only one true God, how can Jesus be God if the Father is God? You yourself said that He is God's Son. How can He be His own Son?" The man spoke kindly, as though he were gently reproving a child. He obviously didn't want to appear threatening to Gail.

WHAT SHALL I SAY?

Now she didn't know what to say. She knew that Jesus was God, and she knew He wasn't the Father, but she also knew that she didn't believe in more than one God. And then there was the Holy Spirit. He wasn't the Father or the Son, but He too was God. How could she explain all of this? Maybe she could just change the subject and ask her Sunday school teacher later. "But you also don't believe that when we die we go to heaven. You don't believe that man has a spirit. The Bible is pretty clear on that, isn't it?" Gail hadn't meant to add that questioning note at the end, but the man's quick Bible knowledge had startled her. She had thought that Witnesses just read their magazines. She didn't know that they studied their Bibles.

This time the woman answered, smiling and responding, "Of course we believe that man has a spirit. Ecclesiastes 7:2 tells us, though, that death is the destiny of man, and not some imaginary heaven with wings and clouds. And Ecclesiastes 9:5 teaches that the dead know nothing, that they have no further reward. We do not serve Jehovah in order to earn some heavenly retirement; we serve Him as well as we can in this life because we know it pleases Him. We do believe that man has a spirit, but not an immortal spirit."

"These matters are very interesting and very important to us. Our magazine and this book, *The Truth That Leads to Everlasting Life,* will answer all your questions on these and other topics. If you would like, we will leave them with you and come back when your husband is home to study the Bible with us. Here," the man said as he offered her the book and magazine.

Gail felt completely defeated. It had seemed so easy when her Sunday school teacher had explained it. She should never have answered the door. She mumbled, "No, I don't want your books. I know what I believe and I'm happy the way I am. I have to go now. Thanks for stopping by." She closed the door slowly, watching the two walk down the sidewalk. "If only I had answers that they and I could both understand when they come to the door!"

THERE ARE ANSWERS!

There are answers to the cultists at your door! Solid Biblical answers exist to the questions they bring. You can have answers for your own faith and answers to the challenges which cults present to Christians. The chapters in this book are designed to give you those answers in understandable language. You don't have to be a professional theologian to share the gospel competently with the typical cultist. In this book you will learn how to deal with Jehovah's Witnesses, Mormons, Moonies, Hare Krishnas, and The Way. In addition, you will find principles that you can use to witness to cultists from other groups.

Our basic premise is quite simple: we believe, after ten years in the field of cult apologetics, that people start and join cults because they have personal needs that aren't being met in traditional churches. Such people think that the cult can meet those needs. Cults always offer to meet such personal needs, and they may appear to meet those needs for a while, but since the cults are only counterfeits of the true gospel, they ultimately leave the cult followers with the same unfulfilled needs. Jesus Christ is waiting to meet those cultists and bring them to complete fulfillment in service to Him. As Christians each one of us has been commissioned to bring the good news of God's salvation to others (Matthew 28:19). We can do this with the simple truth of the gospel contained in God's perfect Word, the Bible.

The counterfeit truths of the cults are like the water that Jesus spoke of in John 4:10-14; it satisfies the body, but only for a short time. He declared, "Everyone who drinks this water will be thirsty again, but whoever drinks the water I give him will never thirst. Indeed, the water I give him will become in him a spring of water welling up to eternal life." (John 4:13,14).

As Christians we have the honor and the obligation to be vessels to others of that spiritual water. Jesus declared, " 'If a man is thirsty, let him come to me and drink. Whoever believes in me, as the Scripture has said, streams of living water will flow from within him.' By this he meant the Spirit, whom those who believed in him were later to receive" (John 7:37-39).

In this chapter we will describe some of the reasons for the existence of the cults, and we will also provide understandable, Biblical remedies to the problems of the cults. For the purposes of this study, we define the general word "cult" to mean a group of religious people who follow teachings and practices that deviate significantly from historic Christianity and the central doctrines of the Bible. A cult is usually founded and led by a single person or a small and "spiritual" elite. The peculiar teachings and practices of the group can continue after the founder's death. We are not using the term "cult" in a derogatory sense, but only as it refers to aberrant teachings and practices—teachings and practices that are not Biblical. Cults either claim to be Christian and Biblical or say that they are at least compatible with Christianity.

There are three main reasons why cults are born: faults within the church, wrong responses to world problems, and wrong motivations of people who become cult leaders or cult followers.

THE WEAKENED CHURCH

The church of the New Testament was very different from the typical American church of today. Because of persecution, Christians in New Testament times had only each other for support at the human level, and therefore each Christian's commitment to Christ had to be very real. Because of challenges at every turn, Christians had to seriously consider their allegiance to Christ in all aspects of their lives. The New Testament church was a close-knit community of believers, bound together by a common faith and a common hope.

Today the visible church is vastly different. In many cases the church has become little more than a social institution, doing its little part in providing Americans with security and entertainment. Although there are individual churches which closely reflect Christ's mandate for the church in the New

Testament, many churches have succumbed to one or more of what we identify as the five major faults within the church: a rise of liberalism, an isolation from contemporary world issues, a lack of sound Bible teaching, a failure to promote a solidly Biblical world view, and a fundamental failure to meet people's spiritual, psychological, and social needs.

Liberalism

With the rise of secular humanism in society as a whole, the church was faced with the need to respond to such teaching. Although some churches have faced this challenge openly and with a strong Christian commitment, most churches have fumbled in their attempts.

Those churches without a strong commitment to the Bible as the Word of God had no absolute answers to the claims of the humanists—that man is the product of a long evolutionary process motivated by chance, that survival of the human race is the supreme goal of civilization, and that man is a machine that possesses no eternal spirit and differs from other creatures only in degree of sophistication. In such churches the Bible has become less important than the opinions of men, and social action has become more important than preaching the gospel. "Fitting in" has become more important than standing on the unique claims of Christ. Members of liberal churches cannot look to their churches for reliable spiritual guidance or for any absolute standard of morality, belief, or conduct. And so some members turn to the cults for that absolute answer.

World Issues

Almost simultaneously with all of this, religious isolationism has been occurring as a reaction against liberalism.

Those churches with a strong commitment to the Bible as the Word of God saw such liberalism as a danger to the very life of the church. Refusing to compromise with humanism, some churches retreated almost completely from all secular challenges. Rather than meeting such challenges head-on and contending for the faith (Jude 3; 1 Peter 3:15), some churches ignored the challenges almost to the point of denying the existence of the outside world.

In some ways they became like the Pharisees of Jesus' day, who went to unbiblical extremes to avoid offending even a tiny point of the law. If the Bible commanded a tithe of 10 percent of the harvest, the Pharisees tithed even their small supplies of spices (Matthew 23:23). Our modern "Pharisees" see that the Bible rejects compromise with the world, so with misguided zeal they simply tune out the world. But in doing so they all too often ignore the emotional, psychological, and spiritual needs of their members—people who cannot forget that the world exists but who want Biblical help in dealing with the world. Jesus wisely observed, "You give a tenth of your spices—mint, dill and cummin. But you have neglected the more important matters of the law—justice, mercy and faithfulness. You should have practiced the latter without neglecting the former" (Matthew 23:23).

Some members of these churches, realizing that they were not getting adequate answers in church to the challenges of the world, turned to the cults for those answers. Even though the cults' answers are ultimately unsatisfying, the cults are willing to meet the world's challenges head-on without backing down on their own brand of belief.

Bible Teaching

As Protestant belief was broken down into liberal and fundamental segments, sound Bible teaching suffered. It is true that *some* churches have successfully met the challenges of today with Biblical teaching and Biblical responses. But all too many churches have succumbed to one extreme or the other and thus have sacrificed solid Biblical teaching and practice.

The cults, on the other hand, claim to offer the Bible's "true" interpretation on all matters. Church members who are unsophisticated in Biblical interpretation all too often fall prey to the sinister interpretations of the cults.

World View

The members of most churches in America today are not taught a comprehensive, Biblical view of the world. We are taught that there is a whole list of "bad" things and a whole list of "good" things, but the contents of the two lists are learned piecemeal. There appears to be no rhyme or reason to what the Christian position in any given situation should be.

We should be taught from God's Word to view all of life from the same consistent, unified, Biblical world view. The Apostle Paul states the importance of such a world view: "So from now on we regard no one from a worldly point of view. Though we once regarded Christ in this way, we do so no longer. Therefore, if anyone is in Christ, he is a new creation; the old has gone, the new has come!" (2 Corinthians 5:16,17).

People without such a view cannot protect themselves from the attacks of the cults. Some Christians have learned a limited number of "Biblical" responses to a limited number of specific problems, but they have not incorporated their Christianity into all areas of their lives. Without a pattern of thought and action based on a comprehensive outlook, they cannot combat attacks that they have never encountered before. Such people are susceptible to the cults and are often ensnared by them.

People's Needs

A major cause of the rise in cultism today is the church's failure to meet the emotional, psychological, and social needs of its people. Some churches are responsive in this area, but all too many churches fail to adequately meet the needs of the whole person (James 2:14-17) and are putting their members in danger of being ensnared by the cults.

Most of the attractions of the cults involve such needs. For example: "Join the Jehovah's Witnesses for a sense of belonging." "Join the Mormons for a great family life and security from physical needs." "Join the Moonies and get the satisfaction of knowing you are working for God." "Join the Hare Krishnas and chant your problems away." "Join The Way and have communities of believers all over the world accept you." Join the cults and your problems are solved—that is the theme!

WORLD PROBLEMS

Another factor in the growth of the cults is an increasing awareness by many people of the world's pressing problems. The Jehovah's Witnesses capitalize on this—they begin almost every witnessing situation with a comment about how the awful world conditions are signs that the end is rapidly approaching and that serving Jehovah is the only remedy. When world problems seem to rise higher than any human solutions, the individual often turns (understandably) to superhuman solutions. But without a solidly Biblical world view, the superhuman solutions are often cultic. Someone faced with problems of global proportions often feels insecure and uncertain about the future. The cults offer their own brands of security and a guarantee of future protection for all obedient members.

Still another factor concerns the rise in popularity of relativism in all areas of American society. Too many people have bought the line that there are no absolutes or certainties in this life or the next. Anything is possible but nothing is for sure. No one has any real answers. Religion can provide no certainties. Faced with a world full of uncertainties, many people retreat to the first safe haven they find, where authorities tell them that there *is* ultimate truth, that there *are* certainties, and that allegiance to the cult is one's guarantee that he will be given those certainties.

Each of these factors plays a significant part in shaping an American society conducive to the growth of the cults. Secular humanism strips individuals of a solid Christian background from which to judge their life experiences; fear of the world's problems chases them to havens of safety in the cults; and a reaction against relativism makes them hungry to swallow almost anyone's brand of dogmatism.

PERSONAL REASONS

Cult leaders and cult followers have their own personal reasons for leading and joining cults. Some reasons they share in common and some are unique to each group. Identifying such reasons is the first step toward reaching cultists effectively with the gospel.

Cult Leaders

The one term that would best describe most cult leaders is self-centeredness. Each of the other characteristics we will mention is related to a cult leader's basic self-centeredness. We should remember that the Bible tells us that every person is self-centered before he is born again (see Romans 3:9-20). Instead of being judgmental of those whose lives are self-centered, we should be grateful to God that those of us who are born again are no longer self-centered but are Christ-centered, and that this has taken place only through the grace and power of God (2 Corinthians 5:16,17). When a person is self-centered, he is unable to see worth in others and is unable to act in the best interests of others. He sees others as objects he can use to further himself. Most cult leaders display little concern for the individual but a large amount of concern for their own well-being and status, both within the cult and in society itself.

One aspect of self-centeredness is a refusal to submit to God's will. Although cult leaders claim that their particular cult is the only organization on earth that is following God's will, such leaders show a personal disregard for God's will. We talked with one Jehovah's Witness over a two-year period. Finally one night he suggested that we not meet anymore. We knew that he hadn't answered our challenges on his doctrinal beliefs, so we asked him why he didn't want to meet anymore. He replied, "I'd never tell the brothers this, but as you know, I'm one of the leading elders at my Kingdom Hall. I've worked hard to get where I am. The people look up to me and respect me. They do what I tell them to. I'm not about to trade that power for anything else. Just let me alone. You might be right, but I don't want to know about it." Power had become more important to him than God's will.

Often a person's insecurity is manifested by an overinflated ego. The cult leader frequently tells himself and others that he is the most important individual on earth. Although referring to himself in humble terms, he makes sure that all of his actions and pronouncements enhance his image as a man uniquely chosen by God to lead God's people in these last days. One cult, which claims no leader, is actually led by a man who is "just one of the brothers" but whose teachings are studied alongside the Bible and who is compared to the Apostle Paul. For this cult he is God's man on earth today.

Since the cults we discuss in this book are religiously centered, it is not surprising that most cult leaders have their ministries endorsed by "revelation" from God. If such a leader is really the most important man on earth today, then certainly God must recognize and approve this fact by the man's public "calling" or "revelation." No one can argue with a person's importance if God approves of him! This has the added benefit of forcing all who want to know God's latest instructions to come only to the cult leader. He becomes the mediator between God and men, contrary to 1 Timothy 2:5.

Finally, most cult leaders' insecurity includes a fear of other people and other people's opinions of them. This fear of people is translated into a compelling desire to rule other people's lives. For example, in the Unification Church marriages are arranged by the church, and members must submit to the marriages so arranged. Usually the marriage partners do not even meet until their formal engagement in a church ceremony. Cult members from different cults have often told us that they had been taught to believe and obey whatever the leadership said, even if it was known to be wrong.

These five personal motivations of cult leaders are interrelated, and they work together to produce leaders who are autocratic and dictatorial. From a basic feeling of self-centeredness, a cult personality can rise to the position of divinely-endowed despot.

Cult Followers

Some of the same problems that cult leaders face are also faced by cult followers. The difference is in the ways that leaders and followers cope with these problems. As a generality we can say that while cult leaders handle their insecurity by asserting themselves forcefully and denying their insecurity, cult members handle their insecurity by wallowing in it and allowing themselves to be ruled by those whom they feel are more worthwhile persons.

All of us are products of the original fall of mankind. All of us have some emotional or personality problems. However, those of us who have submitted our lives to God in a personal relationship to Christ have decided that our problems will be evaluated and solved within a Christian and Biblical context. Those who join the cults are also searching for answers to their problems, but they have not found those answers in God's Word.

Sometimes people turn to the cults for answers because they have never received a good Bible background and have never adopted a solidly Biblical view of the world around them. When faced with problems in themselves or in the world, they are unable to recognize Christian answers. One of the best preventive measures to insure that your children do not join cults is to give them a Bible-based, Christ-centered home life that will prepare them to face all the problems of the world with a confident Christian commitment.

A person does not usually join a cult because he has done an exhaustive analysis of world religions and has decided that a particular cult presents the best theology available. Instead, a person usually joins a cult because he has problems that he is having trouble solving, and the cult promises to solve these problems. Often these problems are emotional. We talked to a young man who had just left the Army, hadn't been discharged a week, and had already joined the Children of God (the Family of Love) and had given them 100 dollars. He said that he was lonely, wanted to serve God, and didn't know where to go or what to do. The Family of Love seized on his loneliness, smothered him with love and attention, and almost secured his permanent allegiance. Fortunately his mother called us and we talked to him, and within an hour he saw how wrong the cult was and decided not to join. We urged him to join a good, small Bible study and to become involved in a strong church. Without a good Christian foundation and close relationships with other Christians, he would still be a candidate for the cults.

Insecurity is one of the biggest problems of people who join cults. Unlike cult leaders, cult followers readily admit their insecurity. However, rather than building themselves up to overcome their insecurity, they reinforce their low self-images through their commitment to the cult and its leadership.

This insecurity can be manifested by a low self-image, which causes the follower to continually talk about how he and everyone else is insignificant and unworthy of the love and attention of the cult leader and/or of God.

Insecurity is also manifested by the person's need to be dominated and directed. He does not feel that he is good enough to make his own decisions, and he does not feel important enough to make decisions about others. For example, Jehovah's Witnesses conduct book studies and magazine studies in which members do not have to think for themselves. At the end of each chapter or article questions are printed which can be answered by parroting back parts of the preceding chapter or article. Everything is done for the members.

Such insecurity can lead a person to think that God wants nothing to do with him as an individual. He isn't good enough for God to care about individually. This produces a need to work for God's approval (all cults emphasize the importance of works in connection with salvation) and a need to secure a relationship to God through an intermediary organization and/or divinely ordained leader. While God may not think them worth caring for, perhaps they can receive His favor by their relationship to "His Chosen People." It is unfortunate that so many people fail to see the great love that God has for each of us. Jesus reminded us, "Do not worry, saying, 'What shall we eat?' or 'What shall we drink?' or 'What shall we wear?' For the pagans run after all these things, and your heavenly Father knows that you need them. But seek first his kingdom and his righteousness, and all these things will be given to you as well. Therefore do not worry about tomorrow, for tomorrow will worry about itself. Each day has enough trouble of its own" (Matthew 6:31-34).

REAL ANSWERS FOR THE CULTS

We have not discussed all the reasons why people join cults, but we have surveyed some of the most important reasons. Some of the fault lies with the churches, some with our changing society, and some with individuals. What we shall see as we examine some of the most prevalent cults today is that their causes are myriad and their membership in the millions. But more important than the *causes* of the rise in cultism is our *response* to it.

There are answers for the cults. There are ways of reaching cult leaders and followers. It is possible for a cultist to come out of his cult and to find new life in Christ. Churches and individuals can cooperate in providing answers to the cultists.

Churches can provide the solid instruction in the Word and the soul-sustaining nourishment that their members need. By facing the challenges of the world openly and with the Word of God, the church can work effectively to reduce the lure of the cults and to help its members grow into Christian maturity.

As members of our American society, we need to be aware of the sales techniques of the cults. While claiming to speak and act for God, cults actually act in spiritual competition to the God of the Bible. We need to beware of wolves in sheep's clothing.

Once we were talking to a young girl who was joining the Mormon Church. Partway through our discussion she blurted out, "Why are you doing this, anyway? Don't you think people have a right to believe whatever they want to?" We responded, "God and our constitution both preserve our freedom to believe whatever we want to. But this doesn't mean that everything and anything is just as true as everything else. Since Mormonism and the Bible contradict each other, both of them cannot be true. However, we believe that each person has the right to make an informed commitment to a religious group. If, after you've heard exactly what Mormonism really stands for, and after you understand that Mormonism and the Bible contradict each other, you still want to join the Mormon Church, then we would respect you for your choice and support your right to make such a decision, even though we believe that it is erroneous. Just don't decide to join before you know what you are joining."

By the end of the evening the girl decided not to join the Mormon Church. She gave her life to Jesus Christ and today is a mature Christian and an integral part of the church. Remember: if you are aware of what a cult really teaches, you are much less likely to succumb to its lures.

We can take action as individual Christians against the rise of the cults. We don't all have to be professional theologians. We don't all have to be linguists specializing in Hebrew and Greek. We don't all have to be experts on each of the thousands of cults in the United States.

The answers to the cults are found in the Bible and are displayed in a committed Christian's life. Effective answers to the cultists are those answers which show that the cult is not meeting the needs of the cultist, but that Jesus Christ is meeting those needs in our lives. In the following pages we will discuss what the cultists are taught, and we will provide

Biblical answers to these teachings. As we grow in our Christian commitment, our effectiveness as a testimony to the power of God grows also. The weapons against cultic warfare are the tools of the successful Christian life. Paul urged us to "Put on the full armor of God so that you can take your stand against the devil's schemes." He identified that armor as "the belt of truth buckled around your waist, with the breastplate of righteousness in place, and with your feet fitted with the readiness that comes from the gospel of peace." He also urged, "In addition to all this, take up the shield of faith, with which you can extinguish all the flaming arrows of the evil one. Take the helmet of salvation and the sword of the Spirit, which is the Word of God" (Ephesians 6:10-17).

STOPPING THE CULTIC EXPLOSION

The growing proliferation of the cults can be stopped. It is possible for cultists to be saved. Gail, the woman we met in the beginning of the chapter, called us just after the Witnesses left her house. "They had an answer for everything I said. I couldn't get anywhere with them. I should never have answered the door." We talked with her for nearly an hour, even though she was calling from over a thousand miles away. We showed her that there are solid Biblical answers, that cultists can be saved, and that it is possible to give the cultists at the door a sound defense of the faith while at the same time extending the love and acceptance of Christ.

Churches can take an active role in stopping the growth of the cults. First, and most important, churches can provide for the very real personal needs of their own people and for people outside the church. Jesus instructed us to provide for each other and those in the world, and our enthusiastic response to that command can do much to build healthy Christians who are impervious to the lure of the cults and are able to minister effectively to those around them.

Individuals like you can make a difference in the realm of the cults. The same personal motivation that helps you grow as a Christian can help you learn the Biblical and spiritual answers to the cultists you meet. With a living and vibrant relationship to Christ, and a growing appreciation of the Bible, you can find along with Gail the answers that you need. Today Gail is not a professional "cult-hunter," but she can provide answers to the cultists at her door. You can do this too!

2/ WHAT THE CULTISTS ARE TAUGHT

"Religious freedom must be preserved at all costs. Sure, there are cult leaders who abuse American religious freedom, but they don't do that much harm, and the only alternative is to have government spying on *my* personal worship and beliefs. Besides, only kooks join cults anyway!" Jack hit his fist against the steering wheel for emphasis as he looked at Mark, one of his car pool members, in the rearview mirror.

Mark shook his head adamantly. "They can do a lot of harm to a lot of people. What about Jonestown and the People's Temple? I'd say 913 dead cult followers were certainly harmed! If you think only kooks join, let me tell you something. Remember Joan Clark, head of personnel, who took a three-month leave of absence last spring? She took that leave of absence to look for her daughter, who dropped out of her senior year at Columbia University to join the Moonies. But Joan hasn't heard from her daughter in almost a year. Joan's son just got one letter from the daughter that said she hated her parents and her old life and has devoted everything to Rev. Moon and his wife, her so-called spiritual parents. Her daughter wasn't dumb—she had a 4.0 grade point average when she left school and she was the leader of her church youth group. It affects all of us in one way or another, Jack. I don't think the government should let these religious charlatans get away with it!''

"You're both wrong about some of what you say," said Claire from the passenger side of the front seat. Jack's wrong in saying that only kooks join and Mark's wrong in saying that cult leaders are dangerous. Who says what a cult is, anyway? I know we're all Christians in the car pool, but doesn't everyone have the right to believe whatever they want to? Who are we to tell Joan's daughter that Moon and his wife aren't her spiritual parents? Some people would even call Christianity a cult. We wouldn't want anybody kidnapping us and deprogramming us from Jesus, would we? We should just let people of other beliefs alone. They can believe what they want to. As long as they're sincere and happy, leave them alone. After all, Jesus said that we should love everyone, no matter what they believe. They all believe in God, and that's what really counts. I talked to a Hare Krishna girl at my door over the weekend and she said they respect and honor Jesus Christ. I have no quarrel with that. You men just aren't tolerant enough!''

Gregory, sitting next to Mark, cleared his throat. "What you're all forgetting is that cult leaders and members are people. They have needs and desires just like you do. Don't just bandy them about in your intellectual rhetoric. Care about them. I never told you all before, but until I became a Christian ten years ago, I was a member of a cult. I was a Jehovah's Witness my whole life. I wasn't a kook and I can't say I was deliberately hurt by the cult, but I was a person who was searching for peace with God, and trying very hard to find it as a member of Jehovah's Witnesses. I sure do thank God that a Christian cared enough about me as an individual to share the gospel with me, to show me the love of Christ, and to help me find that long-sought-after peace with God.

"Did you all know that Tom Miller, at the security gate, is a Mormon? Have you ever tried to share Jesus with him? Did you know that he is lonely and scared because he's afraid that he isn't good enough to make the grade in the Mormon Church? He thinks he might be having a nervous breakdown. Do any of you care enough to help?"

The four were silent as they drove into the company parking lot. Jack finally spoke. "Gregory, I don't know how to help Tom. What should I do? What should I say? Can we do anything that will really help him?"

Gregory replied, "The first and most important thing is for you to love Tom and to let him know that you love him and care about him. Let's talk more about it on the way home tonight. I've done a lot of study about the cults, and I think we can all work together to help Tom and others like him."

CULTISTS ARE PEOPLE

Gregory is right—cultists are people with needs and desires just like everyone else. People who join cults do so because they have become convinced that their special needs will be met by the cult. However, once they have committed themselves to a particular cult system, they become bound to adopt that system's unique and warped world view. In this chapter we will look at the cultic world view and discuss four major areas of cultic teaching. We will look at what cultists are taught about the world, what cultists are taught about other religious people (including evangelical Christians), what cultists are taught about doctrine, and what cultists are taught about themselves and their group. Perhaps the most important refrain of the song of the cults is that life is a battle of "us" against "them." As we shall see, everything in a cultist's life is categorized according to whether it is approved by the cult or is a part of the "enemy world."

This chapter will be your key for answering the cults. We will briefly discuss what the cultists are taught in four major areas and will give you the Biblical principles for answering those false teachings. You can use these principles for answering the cultists from the Word of God. As we go on to the specific chapters on specific cults, you will see how these same principles can be used with each of the cults as an effective tool of evangelism.

CULTISTS VERSUS THE WORLD

The "world" for the cultist is anything outside the safe haven of his own cult. If a person leaves the cult he is at the mercy of the evil world. There is no middle ground. Cultists are taught that the world is entirely evil, hopelessly enslaved by Satan, and not to be trusted for anything. The cultist who might feel insecure about his cultic involvement has nowhere else to turn: everyone and everything else, including all other religions, is part of Satan's kingdom. Cultists are taught to fear the world, whereas Christians are taught that perfect love casts out all fear. Cultists are taught to flee the world, whereas Christians are taught to test all things and defend the Biblical faith.

Cultists are also taught that the world will ridicule and reject them for their stand for God. Often 1 Corinthians 1:27,28 is misused to support this idea:

> But God chose the foolish things of the world to shame the wise; God chose the weak things of the world to shame the strong. He chose the lowly things of this world and the despised things—and the things that are not—to nullify the things that are.

Since cultists usually do not study the Bible in context or systematically, they fall prey to the cults' faulty application of this verse (and others), never realizing the true context. An examination of the context (especially verses 20-25) reveals that the crucifixion of Christ is the "foolishness" that the world rejects. It is the Christian's *preaching of the cross* (verse 23) that makes him appear foolish; it is not odd cultic practices, such as Jehovah's Witnesses' refusal to participate in government or to take blood transfusions, or the Hare Krishna's unusual dress and public conduct. It is an honor to be ridiculed for preaching Christ; it is a disgrace to be ridiculed for following some man-made oddity that has nothing to do with God's will.

Cultists are also taught that the world will actively persecute them for their stand with God. Such persecution is not limited to literal and physical persecution, but has been reinterpreted by cult leaders to include any opposition at all. Thus, Jehovah's Witnesses claim that they are being persecuted when a Christian tries to share Christ with them. The Way's followers claim persecution when members' parents keep trying to win their children away from their single-minded devotion to Wierwille's system and to a more reasonable devotion to Christ Himself.

Matthew 24:9 is the favorite verse for "proving" this persecution. Not only is the cultic application of the verse erroneous, but cult leaders often use faulty logic to apply it to the supposed truth of their own system. The verse reads, "Then you will be handed over to be persecuted and put to death, and you will be hated by all nations because of me." Cultists are taught that any opposition which they suffer is in direct fulfillment of this verse. However, the passage is part of Jesus' discourse on the very last days and may not have reference to those who today suffer for the gospel's sake. Also, there are few places in America today where cultists are put to death for their beliefs!

The cults use faulty logic in trying to use this verse to validate their systems. They try to say that the fact of their members' persecution *proves* that their world views and religious or doctrinal beliefs are true. But the verse is not saying this at all. Jesus is not saying that *only* His true followers will be persecuted, or that persecution will follow *only* true believers. Persecution is not necessarily a validation of one's message. During World War Two, for example, many people were persecuted by Nazism, sometimes for very different reasons. Evangelicals, Jews, and Jehovah's Witnesses (to name just a few) were all put to death and persecuted. Does that mean that the beliefs of all three of these groups are true? How could they all be true when some of the beliefs are mutually exclusive? No, persecution does not validate one's beliefs. Only as we compare our beliefs to the Bible, God's Word, can we determine their validity.

One of the strongest motivations that a cultist has for staying in his cult is the threat of divine judgment and destruction on him if he leaves "God's organization." Usually this threat is coupled with a strong end-of-times stand on the part of the cult. The "end" of all things is just around the corner, God will destroy the unbelieving world, and only the faithful cult members will be spared to enjoy God's favor. Matthew 24 again supplies a favorite misused Bible text. Often cults will point to the parable of verses 45-51 as a picture of what will happen to those who are faithful to God (in the cult) and those who will be cut to pieces by God (everyone else). In fact, the Jehovah's Witnesses are taught that the Watchtower organization is the "faithful and wise servant" referred to in verse 45. While Christians can agree that judgment is coming on the world and all its inhabitants, we have some objective criteria for determining whether we are on God's side or the world's side. The Lord does not require allegiance from us through blind fervor. We do not serve Christ out of fear, but out of love (Romans 5:8). One's fear of coming judgment should not drive him to false protection from a cult that contradicts the Word of God. Instead, one's fear of coming judgment should drive him to the arms of Jesus Christ (Matthew 11:28-30), resting upon the promises of his Word (Luke 24:44-49), confident that He does not desire to condemn anyone (Matthew 23:37-39; Ezekiel 18:32).

CULTISTS VERSUS OTHER RELIGIOUS PEOPLE

The cultist at your door already considers you outside the realm of God's influence, since God only works within his particular system. It is only possible to have God's favor if you are part of His organization, and therefore you are an outsider to God's family.

As a Christian, you are a special kind of outsider. Depending on your attitude to the cultist's message, you are either a lost and blind sheep, duped by your religious superiors, or you are one of those religious superiors, a ravenous wolf, drawing others to destruction with you.

The innocent religious person is misguided, ill-informed, and duped by the clergy, who are partners with Satan to deceive innocent people. Such an innocent person is ripe for the cultist's message. He is just waiting for someone to release him from the spell of the clergy and bring him into the fold of the cult. This innocent person may have faulty beliefs, but they are not his fault. As long as he is receptive to the cultist's message, he is redeemable.

In actual practice, this translates roughly to mean that the gullible are fair game. We talked with a Jehovah's Witness one evening as he was trying to explain to us why he didn't want to talk to us again. We were trying to set up another meeting, telling him that if he was right he had an obligation to share his truth with us and we had an obligation to examine what he said very carefully. Conversely, if we were right, we had an obligation to share with him and he should test what he said against God's Word. Finally he said, "You have to understand. I don't have time to talk to everyone. I have to make choices. There are basically three kinds of people in this world—the gullible, the reasonable, and the dogmatic. I only have time for the gullible and the reasonable." We asked him how he could determine that we were dogmatic instead of reasonable. He answered, "If you believed what I said, that would make you reasonable." He was unable to explain to us the practical difference between gullible and reasonable.

As Christians, we can't afford to be gullible. We are to test all things (1 Thessalonians 5:21,22; Galatians 1:8-10; Acts 17:11) and actively promote the gospel (1 Peter 3:15). When someone's salvation depends on it, we cannot afford to play "innocent," hoping that by not disagreeing with the cultist we will somehow win him to Christ. If by our silence we are failing to tell the cultist what the Word of God says, how do we propose that he is to hear it? Cultists only come to Christ because Christians are willing to tell them the truth, to show them the love of Christ, and to challenge them to examine their faith in the light of the Bible. As Christians we cannot afford to be classified as harmless innocents who have been duped by religionists.

Cultists are taught that if a contact is not "gullible," he is probably an emissary (literal or otherwise) of Satan, actively working to take others with him to destruction. The Mormons believe that there is a special place after death just for Satan and such "workers of iniquity." Jehovah's Witnesses call them "evil slaves."

Our most important response as Christians to such faulty labeling is to show the cultist that we do not fit the description that he has been given. We were talking with some friends in a restaurant about one cult we were researching. The people at the table behind us happened to belong to that cult. They came over to our table and started telling us that their group was not cultic at all and that some terrible people, the Passantinos, were all wrong about what they said. We talked quietly with them for 15 or 20 minutes, sharing the gospel with them lovingly but firmly. We showed them that we respected them and had a genuine concern for their welfare. They seemed to enjoy talking with us, and so we asked if they would like to talk again in a more comfortable setting. They had tentatively agreed when we handed them a business card with our name and phone number on it. When they realized that we were "the terrible Passantinos" they refused the card, turned abruptly, and started to leave. We tried to get them to stay, telling them that we weren't that terrible and really did want to talk earnestly, but they refused to listen anymore. Their indoctrination against us, whom they had never met before, forced them to reject us and our message. Our point is that your interaction with a cultist should be so different from what he has been led to expect that he will be willing to sit down and really consider the Scriptural truths you have to share. Behave in such a way that they will not consider you "the enemy."

CULTISTS AND DOCTRINE

Although each of the cults has different interpretations of central Christian doctrine, most of the cults follow traditional deviations of one form or another. Ten years ago, when we extensively studied early Christian heresies, we found that almost every doctrinal deviation held by the cults today was held by other cults in the first four or five centuries of the Christian church. Reading an account of the heresies in the early church reads like a catalog of the beliefs of the major cults today. Let's look at the most common misinterpretations of essential doctrine in the areas of the Bible, God, Jesus Christ, mankind, and salvation.

The Bible

Every cult reduces in some way the absolute and final authority of the Bible. The Unification Church claims that the Bible is not complete, The Way claims that it is for a past time, Jehovah's Witnesses cannot interpret it without Watchtower literature, Hare Krishnas consider it one of many holy scriptures, and Mormons do not trust its translation and add other scriptures to it.

This cultic attack on God's Word takes two fronts. On one front, the Bible itself is considered faulty. It may be incomplete, for another time period, corrupted in the early centuries of the church, or a mixture of God's Word and man's word. On the other front, cults almost always supply the "something extra" that is needed to bring us God's will perfectly. The Bible isn't good enough as it stands—we need something else. The Jehovah's Witnesses are given the Watchtower organization, called the "faithful and wise servant," who gives "meat (interpretation) in due season" to the faithful followers. The Unification Church learns God's will for today from the anointed utterances of Rev. Moon. Hare Krishnas are taught from the many sacred writings of Hinduism, along with a smattering of Western sacred texts, including parts of the Bible. Mormons add the sacred scriptures in the form of *The Book of Mormon, The Pearl of Great Price, Doctrine and Covenants,* and the inspired utterances of the church president-prophets.

Hebrews 1:1,2 shows us the all-sufficiency and supreme importance of the Bible as the standard of divine truth: "In the past God spoke to our forefathers through the prophets at many times and in various ways, but in these last days he has spoken to us by his Son, whom he appointed heir of all things, and through whom he made the universe."

God

First John 5:20 tells us the importance of correctly identifying God: "We know also that the Son of God has come and has given us understanding, so that we may know him who is true. And we are in him who is true—even in his Son Jesus Christ. He is the true God and eternal life." Merely having "faith in God," whoever God is, isn't enough. God has revealed Himself to us in the Bible and in His Son, and we must worship the *true* God to inherit eternal life. The God of the cults is a counterfeit God, a God with no power to save.

Each of the cults has a God different from the God of the Bible. The Jehovah's Witness God is not omnipresent and certainly not triune. The Mormon god is one of many gods, has a material body, is not triune, and has not always been God. The Unification Church God is a God of Eastern duality—male and female, with positive and negative forces; and man is God incarnate. The Hare Krishna God is impersonal, and Hare Krishnas deny the Trinity. The God of The Way International is not triune.

While we cannot understand infinitely who God is, we can know a great deal about His identity. Using the Bible as our guide, we can have confidence that the knowledge we gain from the Scriptures is accurate, although beyond our full understanding. The Bible tells us that God is unique, eternal, immutable (unchanging), omnipotent (all-powerful), omniscient (all-knowing), omnipresent (everywhere at the same time), triune, spirit, and personal.

God is *unique:* there is only one true God (Exodus 9:14; 2 Samuel 7:22; Isaiah 46:9; 1 Corinthians 8:4-6). God is *eternal*: He has no beginning and no ending (Exodus 3:14; Habakkuk 3:6; Deuteronomy 33:26,27). God is *immutable:* He does not change (Malachi 3:6; James 1:17; Isaiah 46:9,10). God is *omnipotent:* all power subsists in Him (Isaiah 59:1,2; Jeremiah 32:17; Mark 10:27; Romans 4:21; Psalm 115:3). God is *omniscient:* everything is known by God (1 John 3:20; Psalm 94:10,11; Isaiah 40:13,14). God is *omnipresent:* no location can escape His presence (Jeremiah 23:23,24; 1 Kings 8:27; Psalm 139:7-12). God is *triune:* within the nature of the one true God are three eternally distinct divine Persons (Titus 1:4, cf. John 1:1,14; John 20:28; Titus 2:13; cf. Acts 5:3,4 Matthew 28:19). God is *spirit:* He is not a part of the material world (John 4:24; Colossians 1:15). God is *personal*: although one in nature, the Father, Son, and Holy Spirit are distinct divine Persons. God is personal in that He possesses all the necessary attributes of divine personhood (Jeremiah 10:14-16; Psalm 94:9,10; Exodus 3:14).

Jesus Christ

All the cults deny the Biblical Jesus Christ in one or more ways. In fact, the Bible warns us that those preaching false Christs will become more and more numerous as the last days progress (1 John 4:3; Matthew 24:24).

Essential to the Christian faith are the Biblical teachings that Jesus is the Christ, the promised Messiah; that He is one in nature with the Father (He is God); that He was truly incarnated as man; that He rose bodily from the dead; that He will return at the end of the age to judge all men; and that He saved us from our sins on the cross. Denial of any of these essential teachings is a denial of Christ Himself.

To the Hare Krishnas, Jesus is an enlightened one, but only an avatar, or personal manifestation of the impersonal God. The Jesus Christ of the Unification Church is a failure whose incomplete mission is fulfilled by the "Lord of the Second Advent." The Mormon Jesus is the spirit brother of Lucifer, the product of sexual intercourse between God and Mary, and only one of many gods. The Jehovah's Witnesses believe that Jesus is the first and mightiest creation of Jehovah God, a spirit creature who gave up his spirit existence to become only a man, a perfect man who can atone for only some of our sins.

Contrasted to the cultic Jesus Christs, the Jesus of the Bible is supreme and all-sufficient for our needs. He is the Christ, the promised Messiah (Luke 2:11; 1 John 2:22); He is fully God (John 20:28; John 1:1; etc.) and fully man (Philippians 2:5-11; 1 Timothy 2:5). His resurrection was bodily (John 2:19; Luke 24:39) and He will return visibly to judge all men (Matthew 24:30,31; Revelation 1:7; 19:11-15; 20:11-15). Finally, it is to Christ alone that we owe our complete salvation (Acts 4:12; Romans 5:9-11).

Mankind

Most cults also err in their views concerning the nature and destiny of man. Many cults deny that man has an existence or consciousness after physical death (for example, Jehovah's Witnesses), even though the Bible teaches clearly that man is conscious after death (see, for example, Philippians 1:21-24). Many other cultists are taught that man is somehow divine or can become divine (for example, Mormons and Hare Krishnas), even though the Bible makes a clear distinction between the only true God and created man (Romans 1:23; Acts 14:11-18; Ezekiel 28:2-9).

Salvation

In general, cults teach that man is saved by some kind of works. (Some cults teach that man needs no salvation because he is already perfect.) This works-oriented salvation is appealing at first because it seems to give the faithful cult follower a clear path toward salvation. He knows exactly what he has to do to merit God's favor. But disillusionment sets in when the cultist begins to realize that he can never do enough to be absolutely sure that God will accept him. What if the Jehovah's Witness didn't study quite hard enough or conducted one too few book studies, or put in five hours too few in door-to-door work? What if the Mormon didn't participate in enough extra tithes, or didn't do all the temple work that God wanted him to do? Can he ever do enough to be sure? That satisfaction is never reached in cultism.

Cultists cannot rest in the assurance of God's love and forgiveness that we have as Christians (Romans 5:6-11). The Bible explains that the complete provision for our salvation has already been accomplished by Christ, that our only "work" is to "believe in the one he [the Father] has sent" (John 6:29). Biblical salvation is completely apart from our own works: it is the result of the undeserved kindness of God toward us (Ephesians 2:8-10). Christ's sacrifice on the cross is sufficient provision for all sins (Hebrews 7:25-28). Putting our trust in the saving power of Christ's death on the cross for us, we can be "confident of this, that he who began a good work in you will carry it on to completion until the day of Jesus Christ" (Philippians 1:6).

THE CULTISTS THEMSELVES

Although there are thousands of small and large cults in America today, almost all of them teach their members the same things about themselves and about their own group.

Rather than giving members the security of God's immediate approval, most cults teach their members that cult membership only offers an opportunity for salvation. The cultists must work constantly to obtain God's favor and acceptance. Cultists are taught that they cannot come to God except through the cult and/or the cult leader. God does not speak or act directly: He uses the cult and the cult leader as His vehicle of expression. Cultists are taught that they must earn God's favor and that they are in constant danger of not measuring up to God's standards.

This is in sharp distinction to the Bible's teachings, which assure Christians of immediate and direct access to God through Jesus Christ (1 Timothy 2:5). We don't have to fear God because Christians "did not receive a spirit that makes you a slave again to fear, but you received the Spirit of sonship" (Romans 8:15). God is not unapproachable, communicating only through some man-made organization. Paul told those who wanted to know God, "He is not served by human hands, as if he needed anything, because he himself gives all men life and breath and everything else. From one man he made every nation of men, that they should inhabit the whole earth; and he determined the times set for them and the exact places where they should live. God did this so that men would seek him and perhaps reach out for him and find him, though he is not far from each one of us. For in him we live and move and have our being" (Acts 17:25-28). We can be assured of immediate and complete forgiveness of our sins and acceptance by God because "if we confess our sins, he is faithful and just and will forgive us our sins and purify us from all unrighteousness" (1 John 1:9).

The man-made organization of the cult comes between the cultist and God. The cultist is taught that the cult organization is God's restoration of truth on the earth today. It is the only receptacle of God's new revelations for today. It is the only haven safe from Satan's snares and God's judgment. It is the only agency working for the good of mankind.

The cultist is bound so tightly to the group that he eventually believes that reality can only be judged in relationship to the cult. He becomes convinced that the cult leader and the other cult members are the only ones who really care about him. He now owes his life, both physically and spiritually, to the cult, God's organization on the earth today.

As Christians, we are also taught that the "world" outside the church is evil. First John 2:15,16 reminds us:

Do not love the world or anything in the world. If anyone loves the world, the love of the Father is not in him. For everything in the world—the cravings of sinful man, the lust of his eyes and the boasting of what he has and does—comes not from the Father but from the world.

Jesus told us, "He who is not with me is against me, and he who does not gather with me scatters" (Matthew 12:30). However, we do not judge reality by the group or by what some man tells us. We judge reality by what God has revealed to us in His Word. We are to be loyal to our fellowship or church, but not blindly loyal. We do not judge God and His Word by the church; we judge the church by God and His Word. According to the Bible, we are neither to form an allegiance with the world nor to be paranoid about the world.

The answer to what the cultist has been taught about himself and his group is that he himself can come to God and be assured of God's personal love and forgiveness. He is judged on the merits of Christ, and not on his own merits or the merits of his group. Romans 5:17 proclaims that liberation: "For if, by the trespass of the one man, death reigned through that one man, how much more will those who receive God's abundant provision of grace and of the gift of righteousness reign in life through the one man, Jesus Christ."

GOD HAS THE ANSWER

The cultists you will meet on the following pages all share some of the characteristics we have discussed here. But while cultic membership and organization can be discussed in general terms, we must never forget that each cultist is an individual, no matter how much he may try to sublimate his individuality in order to appear the model follower of his cult. He is unique and is known and loved personally by God. Can we, as fellow recipients of God's attention and love, fail to extend the same attitude toward the cultists at our doors?

People join cults for a variety of reasons, and they stay in the cults largely because they don't know that there is anything better. We once talked with a Mormon who seemed very dissatisfied with his life. At the beginning of our conversation he said, "I've talked to people like you before. I've heard all the arguments against Joseph Smith and Brigham Young. Maybe they weren't the best men in the world. Maybe they did have problems. But what am I supposed to do? Even if the Mormom Church isn't right about God, I don't have anyplace else to go. My family and all my relatives are Mormon and I have a real sense of security in the Church. Where else can I find the love and concern that I find from my fellow Mormons? I don't really want to listen unless you can offer me something better!"

Men and organizations are not the ultimate answer. *God* is the only One who can satisfy fully, and a life dedicated to Him through Jesus Christ is the only life that can meet the challenges of the world with the assurance of ultimate triumph.

3/ ANSWERS TO JEHOVAH'S WITNESSES

The pastor's wife answered the door and found a little four-year-old girl shyly holding out a newsprint tract. In a tiny, high voice the little girl squeaked, "Present world conditions are terrible. Jehovah has the answers to the world's problems and I am one of His Witnesses. Would you like this message of truth?" She offered the tract again.

The pastor's wife looked past the youngster to the sidewalk and saw her mother waiting, proud of her daughter's contribution to Jehovah's work. "Honey," began Jane, the pastor's wife, "I love Jehovah too. And I'm so glad He sent His Son, Jesus Christ, to cleanse us from all sin and give us salvation in Him. Did you know that the Bible teaches that Jesus Christ is Jehovah God and that we can be sure of our salvation right now? Jesus loves you dear, and—"

Jane was interrupted abruptly by the child's mother. "We can't talk right now. We have to go to the other houses.

Come on, Sarah, let's go. Leave the tract with the lady."

Jane turned her attention to the mother. "Can't you stay just for a few moments? I would really like to share Jesus with you. You know, you can be born again and have everlasting life with God in heaven. Can't you stay for a moment?"

"We don't need to talk with you. We've heard what Christendom has to say before. We know that Jehovah will take care of us as long as we are doing the work of His kingdom in His organization. We don't want to be born again. We want to live on paradise earth. I want my daughter to have the security of Jehovah's organization. She knows what she has to do to meet God's approval." The girl's mother grabbed her arm and started pulling her down the sidewalk.

"But wait! Don't you know that you don't have to do anything to receive God's approval? Jesus did it all for you. All you have to do is to receive His promise of forgiveness. You can be sure of your salvation right now, today. Please . . ."

It was too late. Jane bowed her head and prayed as the tiny girl ran to keep up with her mother. Jane thought of her own four-year-old, and how she had such a trusting and simple faith in Jesus. He was her Friend who protected her from nightmares, healed her skinned knees, and comforted her when she was sad. Jane thanked the Lord that her daughter knew she could trust Jesus, and she beseeched the Lord on behalf of the little Jehovah's Witness girl, already working for her salvation from an angry taskmaster of a God before whom she needed to earn approval through good works. Jane wrote the little girl and her mother in her prayer book, resolving to pray for them even though they refused to listen to her share the gospel with them. Maybe God could use someone else to reach them.

THE JEHOVAH'S WITNESSES

Almost everyone has had a Jehovah's Witness knock at his door, offering a Watchtower publication and bringing the "news of the kingdom" to anyone who will listen. Out of all the major cults in America today, Jehovah's Witnesses do more door-to-door evangelism than any of them. They believe that they are fulfilling the Biblical pattern which the apostles set in Acts 20:20, where Paul said, "I did not hold back from telling you any of the things that were profitable nor from teaching you publicly and from house to house (Jehovah's Witnesses' New World Translation, abbreviated as NWT).[1]

While door-to-door witnessing can be a very successful method of evangelism, neither this verse nor any other teaches that God's followers can be identified by their door-to-door preaching. The context indicates that Paul was talking to the elders from the church at Ephesus and was telling those believers that he taught *them* "publicly and from house to house." In other words, he instructed the *elders* in the things of the Lord both publicly and *privately*. The context does not refer to going door-to-door evangelizing nonbelievers, but to Paul's private instruction of the church elders in Ephesus.

Jehovah's Witnesses receive their teaching and training from their parent organization, the Watchtower Bible and Tract Society, headquartered in Brooklyn, New York. The Watchtower claims a membership of almost 2.3 million (1981), making it the second-largest of the major American-based cults, behind Mormonism. Known for their distinctive publications, which include the *Watchtower* and *Awake!*

[1] All numbered notes are listed at the back of this book.

magazines, Jehovah's Witnesses dedicate long hours to using these two periodicals as evangelism tools. In 1981, Jehovah's Witnesses distributed 400.8 million copies of the two magazines and 80.6 million other Watchtower publications. False doctrine is propagated throughout the world on a massive scale with the aid of the Watchtower's own printing plant. After 102 years of stormy history, the Jehovah's Witnesses still proclaim the "gospel" first advanced by their founder, Charles Taze Russell, although today that "gospel" reaches farther than ever before.

BEGINNINGS OF THE WITNESSES

Charles Taze Russell

The movement later known as Jehovah's Witnesses began with a small Bible study in 1872, led by Charles Taze Russell, a man with no formal religious training who left orthodoxy (he was raised a Congregationalist) because of his aversion to the doctrine of eternal punishment.

Russell was born in Allegheny, Pennsylvania, in 1852. He started his Bible study when he was only 20 years old. The "truths" that Russell shared with the people in his small study were supposed to be the long-lost truths of the Bible, according to the Watchtower, and Russell's work is compared to that of Christ Jesus Himself! The Watchtower publication *Let God Be True* (1946 edition) states, "True, in recent times men such as C. T. Russell and J. F. Rutherford participated prominently in this world-wide work as Jehovah's witnesses, even as in ancient days Christ Jesus, Paul, Peter, John the Baptist, Moses, Abraham, Noah, Abel and many others participated prominently in the work as Jehovah's witnesses."[*][2]

---

*Jehovah's Witnesses call themselves "Jehovah's witnesses."

In 1879, Russell joined N.H. Barbour in publishing a magazine, *The Herald of the Morning* (transformed over the years into the present-day *Watchtower*). However, Russell and Barbour later severed relations, and in 1884 Russell and his followers formed Zion's Watch Tower Tract Society. The first edition of the renamed *Zion's Watch Tower* was only 6000 copies. Russell's followers grew in number, and all subscribed to the teachings of "Pastor" Russell. Those teachings were published by the society and included a series of seven books by Russell, first called *The Millennial Dawn* and later *The Studies in the Scriptures*. These were said to bring more spiritual light to the reader than the Bible itself.[3]

Russell's teachings are the basis for Watchtower theology today. Although the Watchtower states that it does not follow the teachings of any man, even Russell, it interprets the Bible and professes the same doctrines that Russell taught. Russell denied the Trinity, the deity of Christ, the bodily resurrection of Christ, the deity and personality of the Holy Spirit, the existence of hell, and the consciousness of man after death. He taught that all religions and all members of Christendom were in darkness, and that only followers of his teachings were in the truth.

The teaching that Russell is perhaps best known for is the teaching that Christ's return was to be invisible instead of visible, that it occured in 1874, and that the "end of the Gentile times"[4] would be in 1914. The consensus of Russell's writings and sermons was that 1914 would see the Battle of Armageddon, the destruction of the world powers, and the beginning of the millennium. In fact, he declared, "before that date God's Kingdom, organized in power, will be in the earth and then smite and crush the Gentile image (Daniel 2:34)—and fully consume the power of these kings. Its own power and dominion will be established as fast as by its varied influences and agencies it crushes and scatters the 'powers that be'—civil and ecclesiastical—iron and clay.''[5] When this did not happen as predicted, Russell surmised, ''A few more years will witness their [the times of the Gentiles] utter collapse and the full establishment of God's kingdom in the hands of Messiah.''[6] This still allowed Russell's followers to eagerly anticipate the end of the age while Russell refused to admit that he had been wrong. This was the first of many false prophetic speculations by the Watchtower hierarchy.

Russell did not live to see the "utter collapse" of the Gentile nations: he died on October 31, 1916, while traveling home from a California speaking engagement.

Joseph Franklin Rutherford

The Watchtower Society's legal counsel, J. F. Rutherford, was elected to succeed Russell as the spiritual head of the organization. Rutherford was born in Missouri in 1869. He first had contact with some of Russell's followers in 1894 and joined the movement in 1906.

Rutherford was not liked by all members, and some left the society, or were disfellowshipped, forming their own splinter groups, some of which still exist today. Those who stayed with Rutherford worked with him to develop an organization that worked like a machine, doggedly turning out literature and spreading the Watchtower teachings. Obedience by all members was obligatory.

Rutherford continued the date-setting practices of Russell, setting the date of the end of this world at 1925 in his book (published by the Watchtower Society) entitled *Millions Now Living Will Never Die.*[7] The failure of this new prophecy prompted Rutherford to declare:

There was a measure of disappointment on the part

of Jehovah's faithful ones on earth concerning the years 1914, 1918 and 1925, which disappointment lasted for a time. Later the faithful learned that these dates were definitely fixed in the Scriptures; and they also learned to quit fixing dates for the future and predicting what would come to pass on a certain date, but to rely (and they do rely) upon the Word of God as to the events that must come to pass.[8]

Since that time, the society has been more discreet about mentioning specific dates, although Armageddon seems to be "just around the corner" all the time. Strong primary source evidence exists to show that the Watchtower did set the date of 1975 as the date for Armageddon, although the society, with hindsight, denies it.[9]

Rutherford was the Watchtower leader who gave the "faithful ones" their name, Jehovah's Witnesses, in 1931. At a convention in Ohio, the members adopted Rutherford's resolution that they call themselves Jehovah's witnesses, based on Isaiah 43:10. This new name also served to distinguish them from the many splinter groups that had formed after Russell's death.

Rutherford died on January 8, 1942, failing (as did Russell) to see the Gentile nations destroyed in his lifetime.

Nathan Homer Knorr

Just five days after Rutherford's death, Nathan H. Knorr was elected the third president. He was born in 1905 in Bethlehem, Pennsylvania. He became a Witness at 16 and became a full-time worker at 18. He was named general manager of the printing plant in 1932 and joined the corporate board of directors in 1934. He was named vice-president in 1940.

Less is known about Knorr than about his two

predecessors. Under Knorr, all publications were published anonymously, a move designed to draw attention away from individuals and toward the society as a whole. While Russell had identified *himself* as the "faithful and wise servant" of Matthew 24:45, the *society* was now identified as the "faithful and wise servant."

One of the most notable products of Knorr's administration was the Watchtower's own translation of the Bible, published in sections between 1950 and 1961, and called The New World Translation of the Holy Scriptures. While earlier Witnesses had generally used either the King James Version of the Bible or the American Standard Version (1901), the new translation supported Watchtower theology in crucial texts that had posed problems for earlier Witnesses.[†]

Under Knorr the society strengthened its proselytizing efforts and developed successful training programs for producing new workers for Jehovah's Kingdom. Knorr died at age 72 in June of 1977. Like Russell and Rutherford before him, he missed the end of the age, Jehovah not cooperating with the proposed date of 1975.

Frederick W. Franz

Immediately upon the death of Knorr, Watchtower vice-president Frederick W. Franz, born in 1893, was elected to be the fourth president.

Franz was one of the members of the translation committee for the New World Translation, although he apparently holds no degrees in either Greek or Hebrew.

Although Franz's tenure is only a few years old, under his guidance the society has gained over a million members. His

---

[†] See the section on the New World Translation (page 62).

direction has been instrumental in increasing international membership. The Watchtower Society under Franz has mounted aggressive campaigns to provide religious tolerance for its followers in hostile nations, such as Malawi, in Africa, where the Jehovah's Witnesses are outlawed.

TEACHINGS OF THE WITNESSES

Shortly we will discuss the Watchtower doctrines in the areas of God, mankind, and salvation. At this point we will briefly mention some of the other Watchtower teachings that are distinguishing trademarks of the Jehovah's Witnesses.

The Government

"Since their [Jehovah's Witnesses] allegiance is to Almighty God and his kingdom they do not participate in local, national or international elections or politics. . . . Furthermore, being enlisted in the army of Christ Jesus, he cannot desert the forces of Jehovah to assume the obligations of a soldier in any army of this world without being guilty of desertion and suffering the punishment meted out to deserters by Almighty God. . . . Jehovah's witnesses do not salute the flag of any nation."[10]

The Watchtower's arguments against government loyalty by its members is based on the assumption that all Witnesses are ambassadors of God's kingdom and as such are free from any obligation to their "guest" countries on this earth.

While there are good Bible scholars who would argue on both sides of the issue of Christians going to war, solid Biblical interpretation is unanimous in stating that every person is to support his country in its efforts to promote and protect society's welfare. Romans 13 discusses our obligations to our governments, whether local, state, or national. Matthew 5:13-16 urges Christians to work effectively to promote the truth of the gospel among their neighbors:

> You are the salt of the earth. But if the salt loses its saltiness, how can it be made salty again? It is no longer good for anything except to be thrown out and trampled by men.
>
> You are the light of the world. A city on a hill cannot be hidden. Neither do people light a lamp and put it under a bowl. Instead they put it on its stand, and it gives light to everyone in the house. In the same way, let your light shine before men, that they may see your good deeds and praise your Father in heaven.

In the same way, salt that never leaves the shaker or light that is kept under a bowl does nothing for others. Our involvement in our society should promote the truths of God's Word while not compromising our faith.

We should also note that while Jehovah's Witnesses will not participate in government in some ways, they are more than willing to participate in other ways. Witnesses benefit by the protection afforded them by their countries' armies; they use facilities (such as highways and hospitals) funded by their governments; and they appeal to lawmakers whom they had no part in electing to come to their aid in redressing their grievances (such as their appeals to the U.S. government to gain military exemption in the 1930s and '40s and their appeals for the release of their leaders from prison in 1918 and 1919).

Blood Transfusions

"Realistically viewed, resorting to blood transfusions even under the most extreme circumstances is not truly lifesaving. It may result in the immediate and very temporary prolongation of life, but that at the cost of eternal life for a dedicated Christian."[11]

The issue of blood transfusion is important. Critics of the Jehovah's Witnesses often point to their prohibition against transfusions as a death sentence for the Witness who dies without one. Aside from the medical misinformation which the Watchtower promotes concerning blood transfusions, the Bible nowhere forbids them. The major verse raised by the Witnesses, Genesis 9:4, does not discuss blood transfusions, or even "eating blood," as Witnesses like to define blood transfusions. The passage concerns pagan customs of eating live animals. Dr. Havor Montague, in *Jehovah's Witnesses and Blood Transfusions,* says:

> It was only meat in combination with blood or meat with blood in it that was prohibited. If one concludes from Genesis 9:4 that it is wrong to eat blood, then one must also conclude that it is wrong to eat meat. This would contradict Genesis 9:3, which gives man permission to eat meat. Since the word blood modifies the word meat, we cannot construe the passage to mean that the eating of blood itself is forbidden.

A literal translation of the Hebrew of Genesis 9:4 tells us that God has now given man permission to eat animal flesh, but that most of the animal's blood must be drained out, insuring that the animal is dead before it is eaten. Genesis 9:5 reiterates that man was not to eat live animals out of respect for the value of life.

Regarding the other major verse, Acts 15:20,29, used by the Watchtower as banning blood transfusions, Montague summarizes:

> The Watchtower itself establishes the presupposition that the Law of Moses is in no way binding on the Christian, then affirms that Acts 15 refers to the Law of Moses, then misinterprets the clear meaning of the

passage, saying it refers to "eating blood" and blood transfusions, and then inconsistently says that this prohibition is binding on today's Christian!

As an aside on the medical aspects of transfusions, Montague concludes:

Usually when blood is taken for a transfusion, it is taken from the donor's veins and thus contains very little oxygen or nutrients. Instead, it contains primarily waste products including carbon dioxide, urea, etc. The average blood transfusion adds little food value to the recipient. This is not the purpose of transfusions. The purpose is to replace the missing fluids and oxygen-carrying cells so that the body's own system can continue to supply food and oxygen to the body's cells via the transfused fluids. The Watchtower's argument against using blood transfusions for nutrition is groundless.

The Watchtower allows for the injection of blood fractions into a Witness. If that is permissible, then why not separate, divide, the basic blood fluids and cells and then separately transfuse them into the body? When does blood become "not blood for eating"?[12]

We urge you to obtain a copy of Montague's comprehensive book for further, more detailed information on blood transfusions and Jehovah's Witnesses. We have shown enough from the Bible to show that the Witness prohibition does not promote God's Word, although it does serve to promote the Witness's feeling that he is a persecuted minority who will suffer anything for the Watchtower's God, Jehovah.

Holidays

"Thus, while the celebration of birthdays may seem of little consequence, they exalt the creature, making him the center of attention rather than the Creator. . . . Easter, therefore, finds no support at all in the Bible. It is of pagan origin, and therefore displeasing to God. . . .There is no escaping it: Christmas is of pagan origin.''[13]

Certainly the celebration of holidays is of secondary importance when compared with the Witnesses' errors concerning those doctrines central to our faith, the doctrines concerning God, mankind, and salvation.

Briefly, there is nothing in the Bible explicit or implicit that forbids the celebration of birthdays, Easter, or Christmas. Contrary to Watchtower teaching, celebrating a birthday does not constitute worshiping a person. A Christian could certainly celebrate a birthday as a way of showing someone he loves that he is glad that God gave him life and as a way of sharing the memory of a joyous occasion with one's family. The Bible does not command the celebration of Easter, but devout Christians all over the world have picked a special day of the year to remember Christ's atoning death for us and His subsequent glorious resurrection. This is certainly not displeasing to God. In the same way, although we do not know on what date Christ was born, we are daily thankful that He was born and we join with Christians worldwide to remember that most important birth once each year.

"No matter how flagrantly men may abuse this holiday, they cannot rob devout believers of its wonder and glory as expressed by the angel: 'Fear not: for, behold, I bring you good tidings of great joy, which shall be to all people. For unto you is born this day in the city of David a Saviour, which is Christ the Lord' (Luke 2:10,11).''[14]

Witnesses claim that since Christmas and Easter fall on what used to be pagan holidays, they must also be pagan. However, with thousands of religions all over the world, it isn't likely that any date is free from some sort of pagan celebration, past or present. The Christian sees that honoring Christ's birth and resurrection on special days each year, days that used to be pagan days, is symbolic of the personal transformation which the new birth makes in each Christian. If God can take a pagan like me and transform me through the power of the resurrected Christ into something to give Him glory, He can surely do the same thing with a day.

In concluding this section on secondary Watchtower teachings, we must point out that these are peripheral teachings, not essential doctrines. One's salvation does not hinge on any of these. When the Witness at your door brings up the subjects of government, blood transfusions, or holidays, you can use these ready answers to quickly end such discussions and turn to what really matters: the Bible's teachings on God, mankind, and salvation. It is these that determine our salvation, and these doctrines must form the center of our discussions with Jehovah's Witnesses. Don't waste time on peripheral doctrines in your talk with a Jehovah's Witness. Since you have only a limited amount of time to talk, make that time count. Be sure that he or she leaves your door knowing the gospel and the identity of our Lord and Savior, Jesus Christ.

DOCTRINES OF THE WITNESSES

As we discussed in Chapter 2, most of the cults are in error concerning the central doctrines of the Christian faith. This is also true of the Watchtower. According to Watchtower theology, there is no Trinity, Jesus is a created being, His resurrection was only as a spirit, the Holy Spirit is not God and is not personal, man ceases to exist spiritually at death, there is no eternal punishment for the unsaved, and salvation is by works instead of by grace alone. In addition, the Watchtower teaches its followers that study of the Bible alone is insufficient to teach one God's will.

The Bible and the Witnesses

The Watchtower claims that the Bible is fully God's Word and is the only standard for a life pleasing to God: ". . . the religion that is approved by God must agree in all its details with the Bible."[15] However, in actual practice, Jehovah's Witnesses understand everything in the Bible according to preconceived Watchtower interpretations. We witnessed to a Jehovah's Witness girl one time who said that she found it hard to understand the Bible. We suggested that she read her New Testament by herself every day, asking God to help her understand it. She replied that it would be too hard to do that, but that she had read *The Truth That Leads to Eternal Life* six times in the six months she had been a Witness. We advised her that if she had read the New Testament six times in the same amount of time, she wouldn't have had the questions that she did, but she would understand God's will as expressed in the New Testament.

This has been our consistent experience with Jehovah's Witnesses. While the Watchtower pays lip service to the supremacy of the Bible, it requires its followers to spend so much time with Watchtower publications which "explain" the Bible that Witnesses don't really learn the Scriptures; instead, they learn what Watchtower publications have to say about the Scriptures. Russell's claim concerning his *Studies in the Scriptures* can be applied to all Watchtower publications.

. . . Not only do we find that people cannot see the divine plan in studying the Bible by itself, but we see, also, that if anyone lays the "Scripture Studies" aside, even after he has used them, after he has become familiar with them, after he has read them for ten years—if he then lays them aside and ignores them and goes to the Bible alone, though he has understood his Bible for ten years, our experience shows that within two years he goes into darkness.[16]

The Jehovah's Witnesses' New World Translation of the Bible poses other problems. While it claims to be an unbiased and accurate rendering of the original Old and New Testaments, it is full of twisted translations that deny the essential doctrines of the Bible and instead promote the unbiblical doctrines of the Watchtower. (For a thorough discussion of this problem, see *The Scholastic Dishonesty of the Watchtower,* by Michael Van Buskirk.)

Dr. Julius R. Mantey was one of the greatest New Testament Greek scholars. With numerous degrees in Greek and other languages, he taught Greek for over 40 years and authored several books, including the standard classic, *The Manual Grammar of the Greek New Testament* (with coauthor H. E. Dana). Even the Watchtower quotes him as an authority in trying to support their unscholarly translation of John 1:1. We had the blessing of having the late Dr. Mantey as a guest in our home for several days in 1978, and we asked him to give us his authoritative opinion on the trustworthiness of the New World Translation of the New Testament. He wrote the following statement opposite the title page of The Kingdom Interlinear Translation of the Greek Scriptures (the Watchtower edition of the New World Translation New Testament with a Greek-English interlinear text printed alongside):

There are scores of distortions of Greek words rendered into English: e.g., John 1:1; 8:58; Colossians 1:15,16; Titus 2:13; and Revelation 3:14 in this translation. The grammar is atrocious!

On the Watchtower's attempt to use a quote from Dana and Mantey's Greek grammar textbook to support their mistranslation of John 1:1, Mantey wrote: "My grammar was quoted out of context both times." In fact, he wrote to the Watchtower, asking them to stop quoting him out of context and explaining that John 1:1 supports the deity of Christ quite clearly.

Never agree to use the New World Translation in your discussion with a Jehovah's Witness. It is not a reliable translation and has been rejected by the consensus of recognized Bible scholars. However, you don't need to know Greek and Hebrew or have Dr. Mantey stay with you to be able to convince the Jehovah's Witness at your door not to use his NWT. Remember, our goal is to help the Witness think for himself and to go to God's Word alone to find true salvation and the true God through the Lord Jesus Christ.

When we talk to Witnesses who want to use the New World Translation, we say the following: "We believe that Jehovah wrote His Word so that ordinary people can understand it. But the average person today doesn't know Greek or Hebrew, so he has to trust others to accurately translate into his own language what the Bible originally said. There are hundreds of English translations of the Bible. Which one should we use? We could use one that was done by a committee of unknown people with unknown credentials, but in this case there would be no way for us to find out if they were qualified to translate God's Word. Or we could use a translation that was done by a committee of known people with recognized credentials in Greek, Hebrew, linguistics, and history. In this case we can check to see if they were qualified to translate God's Word. Since God is reasonable, and has given us reason to use, which translation do you think we should use?"

The translators of the New World Testament are unconfirmed, except for Frederick Franz, who represented the committee in a legal matter in the 1950s. Franz has no known degrees in any of the fields necessary for accurate Bible translation. The average person would have no way of checking on the New World Translation's translators. But in the case of the New International Version, we can find out just who translated them and what their credentials were. We have not yet met a Witness who, under these circumstances, has been unwilling to consider a recognized, reliable translation.

The God of the Witnesses

"What, then, do the facts show as to the 'Trinity'? Neither the word nor the idea is in God's Word, the Bible. The doctrine did not originate with God."[17]

The word "trinity" does not occur in the Bible, but it is a widely used theological term that accurately describes a Biblical teaching concerning the nature of God. There are many words that we can use to describe beliefs taught in the Bible, even though these specific words may not necessarily occur in the Bible. For example, "theocracy" is a word that is used by both evangelical Christians and Jehovah's Witnesses to describe God's rule on earth, and yet the word "theocracy" does not occur in the Bible at all. Rather, theocracy is a term used to describe a *teaching* that is found in the Bible. Likewise, the *teaching* of the Trinity is Biblical, as we shall see here and when we discuss Jesus Christ and the Holy Spirit.

The Bible teaches us that within the nature of the one true God (Isaiah 42:8; 43:10; 44:6,8; 45:21; 1 Corinthians 8:4-6; Nehemiah 9:6; 1 Timothy 2:5) are three eternal, distinct, divine, Persons (Matthew 28:19; Luke 3:21,22): the Father (2 Peter 1:17), the Word (Son) (John 1:1,14; 8:24,58; Colossians 1:15-19; Titus 2:13), and the Holy Spirit (Acts 13:2; 10:19,20; Hebrews 3:7-11; Psalm 95:6-11; Acts 5:3,4; Hebrews 9:14).

We will not discuss the deity of Christ or the personality and deity of the Holy Spirit in much detail here, since we will discuss those subjects separately below. Here, though, are some general observations concerning the doctrine of the Trinity that will help you in answering the Jehovah's Witness at your door.

Since the Jehovah's Witnesses do not know what the doctrine of the Trinity really is, they are understandably confused about what Christians believe. The Watchtower misdefines the Trinity and then tries to show that such a definition is unreasonable. They say that we believe that Jesus is the Father. From there they argue many variations of the same point: if Jesus is the Father, then 1) how did Jesus pray to Himself in the Garden of Gethsemane, or 2) when Jesus said that the Father sent Him, how could He send Himself, etc.? Remember, when a Witness challenges your belief in the Trinity, if his challenge begins with "If Jesus is the Father, then . . .", it is a meaningless challenge. We do not believe that the Person of Jesus is the Person of the Father. Instead, Jesus, the second Person of the Trinity, prayed to the Father, the first Person of the Trinity.

Another Watchtower misconception of the Biblical Trinity is that we believe in three gods. The argument goes, "If the Father is God, and the Son is God, and the Holy Spirit is God, then you must have three gods!" Again, sticking to our original Biblical definition, we can answer the Watchtower by saying, "We believe that within the nature of the one God there are three divine Persons. We do not believe in three gods, but in one God who exists as three divine Persons." This definition also answers the Watchtower objection that we have a fractured God—that the Father is one-third of God, the Son is one-third of God, and the Holy Spirit is one-third of God. Instead, we believe that *each Person* of the Trinity is *fully God,* and that *all three Persons* partake fully of the one nature of God.

A favorite refrain of the Watchtower is that belief in a Trinity is pagan. The Babylonians, Egyptians, and Hindus, the Witnesses claim, all believe in trinities, and so the Christian Trinity must be pagan. Not only is this argument illogical, but it is not true. It is illogical because there is no necessary correlation between a statement's truth and its being held by many people. Just because pagans believe in trinities (if they do), this is no reason to suppose that the Christian Trinity is pagan. Pagans also believe in the *existence* of God. Does this mean that God cannot exist? No, the argument must be based on *the teaching of Scripture* and not on illogical arguments. Second, the so-called "trinities" cited by the Watchtower from other religions are not like the Christian and Biblical Trinity at all. They are in reality some form of *tritheism,* or belief in *three gods.*

The last of the common Watchtower arguments against the doctrine of the Trinity concerns its "reasonableness." As with most cults, the God of the Watchtower is a simple God who is easy to figure out. He has no mysteries or complexities, and a Jehovah's Witness can easily grasp his simple God who fits neatly into limited human logic. Such a Witness has been taught to challenge Christians by saying that a belief in the Trinity is unreasonable. How, he may ask, can there be three Persons and only one divine nature? If I can't understand all about it, he may go on, it can't be reasonable and therefore it can't be right. After all, doesn't God say in Isaiah 1:18, "Come now, let us reason together"? According to Jehovah's Witnesses, everything has to be reasonable and capable of being understood fully.

We respond as Christians by saying that Isaiah 1:18 is talking about *salvation* and not about the infinite nature of the Almighty. The doctrine of the Trinity is neither illogical nor unreasonable, but its *complete* comprehension is beyond our finite logic and reason. We do not irrationally say that we believe in three gods and one god, or in three persons and one person, but we do logically say that the Bible teaches one true God in three divine Persons. We are commanded to believe what God reveals to us in Scripture even if we cannot understand it fully here and now.[18]

The Jesus of the Witnesses

"The justice of God would not permit that Jesus, as a ransom, be more than a perfect man; and certainly not be the supreme God Almighty in the flesh."[19]

"In other words, he has the first and direct creation of Jehovah God."[20]

The easiest verse we can use to support the deity of Christ in a good translation is John 1:1. Although the Jehovah's Witnesses use various unscholarly arguments to try to support their translation of the verse, all of them are false. None pose any threat to the Christian assertion that John 1:1 teaches that Jesus is Jehovah God.

John 1:1 says, "In the beginning was the Word, and the Word was with God, and the Word was God." But the Jehovah's Witness translation of John 1:1 says, "In the beginning was the Word, and the Word was with God, and the Word was a god" (NWT).

By such translating, the Jehovah's Witnesses have opposed themselves to the clear Bible teaching that there is only one true God (Isaiah 43:10; 44:8; John 17:3; Deuteronomy 32:39). How could God categorically state in these verses that there are no created gods and that there is no god with Him, and yet say, according to the Jehovah's Witnesses, that "in the beginning" there was "a god" with Him? It doesn't make sense.

By this sort of reasoning, Jehovah's Witnesses are actually taught to be polytheistic. (*Polytheistic* means that they believe in more than one god.) The Jehovah's Witnesses are taught that Jesus is a true god, and that Jehovah, who is not Jesus, is another true god who is greater than Jesus. This is polytheism.[21]

Looking at the context of John 1:1, we find in verse 3 that Jesus is said to be the Creator of all things. In fact, the verse emphatically states that "without him nothing was made that has been made." If we divide all existing entities into two classes, created and uncreated, to which class would the Word (Jesus) of John 1:1-3 belong? Obviously He would belong to the class of *uncreated* things. This directly contradicts what the Watchtower says about Jesus, but it harmonizes beautifully with Isaiah 44:24, where Jehovah declares, "I am the Lord, who has made all things, who alone stretched out the heavens, who spread out the earth by myself."

The Jehovah's Witnesses have only a few verses that they use to support their contention that Jesus was created. Coupled with some faulty premises concerning Christ, they constitute all of the Watchtower argumentation against the deity of Christ. The verses which Witnesses are taught actually teach that Jesus is truly Jehovah-God. The two verses from the New Testament taught most often are Colossians 1:15 and Revelation 3:14.

Colossians 1:15, speaking of Jesus, says literally, "He who is the image of the invisible God, the firstborn of all creation . . . ." Jehovah's Witnesses latch onto the phrase "firstborn of all creation" and misinterpret it to mean that Jesus is the first-*created* of all creatures. They say that Jesus is therefore the first and mightiest creation of Jehovah God. To answer them, we must look at the first word in contention, "firstborn." Actually this word, *prototokos* in Greek, means "the preeminent one, the one with priority, the one with the right to rule, or the one with the sovereignty over."

Inserting the Greek definition into the verse and including the verse following, which is part of the same sentence, we see exactly what Paul meant:

He who is the image of the invisible God, the one with the right to rule over all creation, because he created all things.

Instead of teaching that Christ is *created*, this verse shows clearly that he is the *Creator,* or, as the writer of Hebrews says, "Every house is built by someone, but God is the builder of everything" (Hebrews 3:4). This word *firstborn* is used repeatedly in the Bible in its common usage as defined above. In the Greek translation of the Old Testament, in Genesis 25:31-34, Esau sold his "firstbornness" to Jacob. He didn't sell his being the first-one-created, but he sold his *right to rule* over his father's inheritance. In Exodus 4:22 Israel is called the *firstborn* nation. It was certainly not the first nation to come into existence, but it was the nation which was *preeminent in God's sight.*

Jehovah's Witnesses also use Revelation 3:14 to try to support their belief that Jesus is created and is therefore not God. Examined for what it really says, we find that it actually teaches that Jesus is the *Creator* of the universe. The verse says, "These are the words of the Amen, the faithful and true witness, the ruler ("beginning"—KJV and NWT) of God's creation." These nouns are listed as titles of Jesus. Let's examine each one. *Amen*, in Hebrew Biblical usage, is never used of a person unless it is used of Jehovah. In that case it means "the one who will do what he has promised to do." So Jesus, according to Hebrew word usage, would be considered "Jehovah, the one who is faithful in all things." *The faithful and true Witness* is another title used of Jehovah-God. In Jeremiah 42:5 Jehovah is said to be the "faithful and true witness." So again Jesus is equated with Jehovah.

The final title, *Beginning* (KJV and NWT), is also a declaration of Christ's deity. In Revelation 21:6 Jehovah calls Himself the Beginning, meaning that He is the Source or Ruler of all things. The Greek word used here, *arche*, means the beginning, the source or origin, the ruling one. This is the sense in which *beginning* is used in Revelation 3:14. Jesus is said to be the Origin or Ruler or Source of all creation. This means that He is Jehovah, the Creator of the universe—the Ruler, as the New International Version puts it.

Our final verse for consideration is John 20:28. This is a very clear verse in support of the deity of Christ. Thomas clearly calls Jesus "my Lord and my God."

But we have heard many strange interpretations of this verse by Jehovah's Witnesses, none of which are reasonable or Biblical. The most common Watchtower response is, "Thomas was so surprised and startled that he blurted out, 'O my Lord, O my God!' "

But that is a ridiculous interpretation. The text says that Thomas spoke *to Jesus*. As a good rabbi, Jesus could hardly have let Thomas blaspheme the name of God and yet commend him by replying, "Blessed are you, Thomas!" The clear and obvious meaning of the passage, in harmony with the rest of the New Testament, is that Thomas acknowledged that Jesus is both Lord and God.

Most of the Watchtower arguments against the deity of Christ result from just a few faulty assumptions concerning the subject. The most frequent faulty assumption concerns the Son's subjection to the Father. Witnesses argue that the Son cannot share the divine nature of the Father if He is subject to the Father. Verses such as "not my will, but yours" and "the Father is greater than I" are quoted to show His subjection to the Father. Our Biblical answer is that subjection does not deny a sameness of nature. As the second person of the Trinity, Jesus is subject *positionally* to the Father, or is of lesser positional rank. This does not affect His *nature* any more than the rank of private in the Army makes a person less of a human being than his sergeant (see another example in 1 Corinthians 11:3). In fact, Philippians 2:1-11 describes this ranking: how the Son, while sharing the divine nature, subjected Himself to the Father, and, beginning at His incarnation, shared the human nature and died for our sins. His is the true example of humility.

The second-most-common misassumption of the Witnesses concerning the deity of Christ is in pointing to verses referring to Christ's human nature, as if this proved that He could not be God. Again, a careful study of Philippians 2:1-11 shows that Christ, while eternally existing as God, took on an *additional* nature at the incarnation, the nature of a man. But Christ *never stopped being divine* or participating in the divine nature.

The third major area of misunderstanding concerns the Witnesses' concept of death. For them, death is the same as annihilation. When a person dies, his spirit ceases to exist. From that presupposition come questions concerning Christ's deity, such as, "If Jesus is God, then who ruled the universe while He was dead for three days?" Obviously, if death is defined as the separation of the spirit from the body, then there is no problem with saying that Jesus, the God-man, still ruled the universe during those three days.

The Resurrection and the Witnesses

"Christ Jesus comes, not as a human, but as a glorious spirit creature."[22]

"This firstborn one from the dead was not raised out of the grave a human creature, but he was raised a spirit."[23]

The Watchtower not only teaches that Jesus was raised as a spirit creature, but it also teaches that Christ's second coming is to be (or was, in 1874) as a spirit. In fact, it would be reasonable to assume that the Watchtower teaching concerning the nature of Christ's resurrection follows from the early Russell teachings concerning his invisible return in 1874. If the cataclysmic events Biblically associated with the second coming failed to materialize at that time, the only way out of admitting one's failure as a prophet would be to postulate a hidden and invisible return. Such a return would only be possible if Jesus were not raised bodily from the dead. This may be the origin of the Watchtower teaching on the invisible "spirit" resurrection of Jesus Christ.

The two main verses used by the Watchtower to try to substantiate this "spirit" resurrection of Christ are 1 Corinthians 15:45 and 1 Peter 3:18. But neither verse teaches that He was raised as a spirit, and we shall see that other Scriptures teach clearly that His resurrection was *bodily,* with a glorified, incorruptible, and immortal body.

First Corinthians 15:45 reads in part, "the last Adam [Jesus], a life-giving spirit." However, this does not teach that Christ's resurrection body was spirit in nature; instead, it refers to the resurrection life which Christ has secured for all believers through His own glorious bodily resurrection. Rather than contrasting material and immaterial bodies, as the Watchtower would have us believe, the passage from verses 35 through 54 contrasts *corruptible and death-doomed bodies* with incorruptible and immortal bodies. All believers will have bodies like Christ's at their resurrection (1 John 3:2). They will be material and somewhat similar to the bodies which we have on earth now, but they will be incorruptible, immortal, and glorified. While Witnesses try to buttress their position by saying that 1 Corinthians 15:50 ("flesh and blood cannot inherit the kingdom of God") supports their form of resurrection, even a cursory reading of the passage makes it very clear that literal flesh and blood is not at issue here: *corruptibility* is the issue. "Flesh and blood" is simply a metaphor for the body corrupted by sin.

First Peter 3:18 reads in part, referring to Jesus, "He was put to death in the body but made alive by the Spirit ("in the spirit"—KJV and NWT)." Of course, the New International Version translation easily removes the verse from the context of immaterial resurrection.

This passage in 1 Peter is very obscure, and its precise meaning is debatable. As Dr. Mantey commented to us when he visited us, Peter's Greek did not always conform to the most common usage of his day. This passage in particular allows for an ambiguity of meaning that may keep us from learning its precise meaning this side of heaven. Some interpret it to mean, as the NIV translates it, that Peter was referring to the Holy Spirit's role in Christ's resurrection. Others interpret it to mean that Christ's spirit communicated with the dead during the three days that His body lay in the tomb. Still others interpret it to mean that the same spiritual power that raised Jesus from the dead inspired Noah's preaching to the sinners of his day, those who were disobedient to God at that time and who now are in spiritual "prison," awaiting the last judgment. Each of these views (except the Watchtower one) command the respect of competent Bible scholars. None except the Witnesses' view can be dismissed as impossible. That view can be dismissed as impossible because, as we shall now see, the Bible clearly teaches that Jesus was raised in his own newly-glorified body. That there are a number of valid alternatives to the Watchtower interpretation means that the Watchtower cannot prove its teaching on the resurrection from this passage.

On the positive side, Luke 24:36-43; John 2:19; and John 20:24-29 all clearly teach the bodily resurrection of Jesus Christ. In Luke 24:39 Jesus expressly denies that He is a "spirit creature" by saying, "a ghost (or spirit—KJV and

NWT) does not have flesh and bones, as you see I have." In John 2:19-22, Jesus specifically prophesies the nature of His resurrection by saying, "Destroy this temple, and I will raise it again in three days." John tells us that He meant the temple of his *body* (verse 21) and states that this verse was fulfilled at Christ's resurrection (verse 22). Finally, in John 20:24-29 we find Jesus complying with Thomas's test to prove the resurrection: he must actually touch the same scarred body with his own hands. Jesus invites him to do so, and Thomas's response is to worship Jesus as his Lord and his God (verse 28). The Watchtower's excuse that Jesus "manufactured bodies" to substantiate His resurrection makes no sense if His resurrection was not predicted to be bodily. Why would a physical body be proof of a predicted immaterial resurrection? It wouldn't. We must conclude from the Scriptures that Jesus was raised from the dead after three days in His own transformed body, a body that had been glorified, made incorruptible and immortal, capable of penetrating the heavenly realm.

The Holy Spirit and the Witnesses

"As for the 'Holy Spirit,' the so-called 'third Person of the Trinity,' we have already seen that it is, not a person, but God's active force."[24]

The Bible doesn't agree with the Watchtower dogma. It teaches that the Holy Spirit is a divine Person and is in fact Jehovah-God. First we will deal with the personality of the Holy Spirit, and then with His deity.

What is a person? Even dictionaries are vague. Psychologists are not sure of all of the components of personality. However, we can know some things that a personality *isn't*, and we can know some things that a personality *is*. For example, personality is not physical, although it may be manifested physically. Personality is also not one's heritage or ethnic or cultural background. One does not become less of a "person" if he loses an arm or a leg. Personality does include at least intellect, emotion, will, and self-cognizance, or the ability to say "I," to realize one's own existence apart from the rest of the world. Let's see if the Holy Spirit fits these criteria.

The Bible teaches that the Holy Spirit has intellect. In John 16:7-15 the Holy Spirit speaks and is called "the Counselor" (Greek *parakletos,* used also of Jesus in 1 John 2:1). The Holy Spirit is lied to in Acts 5:3 and is tested in Acts 5:9. These things can be done and experienced by a *person* (in this case a divine Person).

Only a *person* can be directly quoted and can call himself "I." This is exactly what the Bible says concerning the Holy Spirit in Acts 13:2. A common Watchtower answer to this might be that this reference to the Holy Spirit is just a personification. However, there is nothing in this context to warrant that presupposition, and when the Bible personifies other things, it does not *directly* quote them. The Holy Spirit is also quoted in Acts 10:19,20 and other verses.

Other actions of personality are ascribed to the Holy Spirit in the Bible. He works (1 Corinthians 12:11), searches (1 Corinthians 2:10), testifies (John 15:26), teaches (John 14:26), reproves (John 16:8-11), regenerates (John 3:5), prays (Romans 8:26), guides (John 16:13), glorifies (John 16:14, and calls (Acts 13:2). Only a *person* can do these things. The testimony of Scripture is clear: the Holy Spirit is a divine *Person.*

Now that we have shown from the Bible that the Holy Spirit is a Person, we need to see if the Bible teaches that the Holy Spirit is also Jehovah-God. We find that the Bible ascribes attributes of the only true God to the Holy Spirit.

The Holy Spirit is said to be eternal (Hebrews 9:14). He is

also the Creator (Job 33:4; Psalm 104:30). In Acts 5:1-4 Peter first says that Ananias lied to *the Holy Spirit*, and then identifies *God* as the One to whom Ananias lied, clearly equating the Holy Spirit with Jehovah-God. In fact, many parallel passages identify first Jehovah and then the Holy Spirit as Jehovah. Isaiah 6:8-10 quotes *Jehovah*, but the New Testament reference to the same passage declares that *the Holy Spirit* was speaking (Acts 28:25-27). Psalm 78:17,18 says that the Israelites sinned against *God*; Isaiah 63:10 says that they sinned against *the Holy Spirit*. Deuteronomy 32:12 says that *Jehovah alone* led His people; Isaiah 63:11-14 identifies the Leader as *the Spirit of the Lord*.

The teaching of the Scriptures is clear: the Holy Spirit is personal and is the third Person of the Trinity. He is Jehovah-God. We spent most of an afternoon one day speaking with a Jehovah's Witness elder about the doctrine of the Trinity, especially talking on the deity and personality of the Holy Spirit. We brought up the information we presented here and much more that space precludes us from discussing here. Just when we were ready to begin talking about the deity of Christ, he said he had to leave. "Anyway," he concluded, "the Watchtower is still right. You may have proved that the Father and Holy Spirit are the one Jehovah-God, but you didn't prove the Son yet. I have to leave." Nothing we could do persuaded him to stay or set another time when we could discuss the diety of Christ. To this day, years later, he is still an influential Jehovah's Witness, unwilling to hear about the third Member of the Trinity. While some Witnesses hear the Biblical truth about the Trinity and leave the Watchtower organization, others won't hear it all and think that their ignorance justifies their remaining in an organization that is not Biblical.

Mankind and the Witnesses

The Watchtower position on the nature of man differs from the teaching of the Bible in one major way: the Watchtower man does not have a spirit that exists after biological or physical death. The unrighteous dead cease to exist for eternity, and the righteous dead are recreated spiritually from Jehovah's memory at the "resurrection." [25]

However, the Bible clearly teaches that man is conscious after death, though his spirit is separated biologically from his body. Ecclesiastes 12:7 reminds us that while the body turns to dust, the spirit "returns to God who gave it." Second Corinthians 5:1-10 states that when a believer's spirit leaves his body at the time of physical death, he is "at home with the Lord" (see verse 7). Philippians 1:20-24 is clear:

> I eagerly expect and hope that I will in no way be ashamed, but will have sufficient courage so that now as always Christ will be exalted in my body, whether by life or by death. For to me, to live is Christ and to die is gain. If I am to go on living in the body, this will mean fruitful labor for me. Yet what shall I choose? I do not know! I am torn between the two: I desire to depart and be with Christ, which is better by far; but it is more necessary for you that I remain in the body.

Matthew 25:46 states the destinies of both the unrighteous and the righteous after physical death: "Then they will go away to eternal punishment, but the righteous to eternal life." As eternal as life is for the righteous, that is how eternal the punishment of the wicked will be. They do not simply cease to exist. [26]

Salvation and the Witnesses

The Watchtower doctrine of salvation is complicated. We

will briefly discuss two areas: the Watchtower type of salvation, and the Watchtower mode of salvation.

There are two types of salvation, according to the Watchtower. "In addition to those 'bought from among mankind as a first fruits' to form that heavenly congregation, therefore, others are to benefit from his ransom sacrifice and gain everlasting life through the removal of their sins and accompanying imperfection. . . . Since those of heavenly congregation serve with Christ as priests and 'kings over the earth,' such other recipients of the ransom benefits must be earthly subjects of Christ's kingdom, and as children of an "Eternal Father" they attain everlasting life."[27]

According to the Watchtower, only a small number of believers will ever go to heaven—the members of the "heavenly congregation." These are the only ones who are born again, the only ones who have "Jehovah's holy spirit" within them, and the only ones with a "heavenly hope." This is in direct contradiction to Scriptures such as John 3:1-18; Romans 8:9-11,16,17,23; 1 John 3:24; and especially 1 John 4:7 ("Everyone who loves has been born of God and knows God") and 1 John 5:1 ("Everyone who believes that Jesus is the Christ is born of God, and everyone who loves the father loves his child as well"). There are not two classes of righteous; there is only one class: those who are saved, born again, and indwelt by the Holy Spirit, inheritors of the promise.

The Watchtower mode of salvation is also complicated. Watchtower publications declare that a person's forgiveness of sins (what we call salvation) is entirely by God's grace on account of Jesus' "ransom sacifice." On the other hand, the Watchtower teaches that this forgiveness is only the beginning of sanctification, which must be actively pursued throughout one's life. It is possible to lose one's forgiveness only once: there is no coming back, and one's destiny thereafter becomes eternal annihilation. "The process of sanctification is not all on one side. Sanctification must be maintained, and in this the believer has a part. He can lose his sanctification or hold on to it. . . . They must maintain their sanctification down to the end of their earthly course. To do this, they must keep clear of dishonorable things and persons who practice dishonorable things, so as to be a 'vessel for an honorable purpose, sanctified, useful to his owner, prepared for every good work' (2 Timothy 2:20,21)."[28]

The practical effect of this teaching on the average Watchtower member is that while he thanks Jesus Christ for the *opportunity* to merit God's favor and be sanctified, he feels compelled to work his way to eternal security. While paying lip service to salvation by grace alone, apart from works, the Watchtower's teaching fosters a belief that salvation is a combination of faith and works. This practice denies the clear Biblical teaching of salvation by grace alone as expressed in such verses as Ephesian 2:8-10; Romans 4:1-8; Galatians 5:1-6; and Philippians 3:1-9.

ANSWERS TO THE WITNESSES

How does the average Jehovah's Witness at your door think? Everything he knows about any religion, including his own, is from Watchtower sources. Constant repetition insures the same responses and beliefs from any Jehovah's Witness around the world. Constant repetition of Watchtower teachings removes the need for the individual to think for himself.

How can you answer the Jehovah's Witness at your door? Always be completely honest. God does not need us to lie for Him. Say that you are a Christian and want to share the true Jesus with him. Do not pay money for his publications.

Either do not take them or say that you do not believe in supporting an organization that is misleading its members. No other topics are as important as the nature of God (the Trinity), the deity of Christ, and salvation by grace. If the Jehovah's Witness at your door has the wrong God, the wrong Savior, or the wrong salvation, he cannot have eternal life. Stick to these topics and do not let him get off the track. Be sure that you are talking in simple enough terms and concepts, ones that he can understand. Never presume that he agrees with you or understands you. Repeat as often as necessary, and keep asking whether he understands.

Some Christians incorrectly use 2 John 9-11 to prohibit cultists from entering their homes under any circumstances. But far from teaching us to totally abstain from any kind of contact with cultists, these verses warn Christians not to be *indoctrinated* by cultists. We should not allow a Jehovah's Witness or other cultist to teach us or preach to us (whether in our homes or elsewhere), but we have an obligation to answer his objections (if sincere) and to preach the gospel to him (1 Peter 3:15).

Although he may say it isn't "loving" for you to be firm and authoritative, it would be completely unloving to let him go to hell because you would not speak up to tell him how to go to heaven. Be sure to present the plan of salvation so that, if he never talks to another Christian, he will still know how to be born again.

And regardless of anything else you do, remember to love the Jehovah's Witness even though you reject what he has been taught. If you cannot love him, and show him the love of God in you, your time has been wasted.

Jody was a Jehovah's Witness woman who felt the love of God through the love of a Christian who was willing to give her answers when she knocked on her door. Here is Jody's story.

LIFE AS A "WITNESS"

Jody was a plump, curly-haired grandmother. She had been asked to tell her story to the adult Sunday school class during the last class of the quarter on evangelism. She had belonged to the church since she had become a Christian 12 years earlier, when the pastor's wife had witnessed to her. Jody had been a Jehovah's Witness for 20 years when she first met the pastor's wife, Clara Guest, during Jody's door-to-door witnessing for Jehovah's Witnesses.

"I became a Jehovah's Witness as a young housewife 32 years ago," she began. "I was home during the day while my husband worked, and, coming from a large family, I wasn't used to all that time alone. After a few months in our new town, I started dreaming about what I wanted our new family to be like. I wanted lots of kids, a nice house with enough room in back for a swing set, and nice family outings. I used to picture what our family would look like, all dressed up on Sunday morning, walking out the door to church. I wasn't even pregnant yet, but I pictured my husband and me leading six children off to church on Sundays!

"The only problem with my dream was that it was just a dream. We didn't have any children, and we didn't go to church. I asked my husband, Bill, to go a couple of times, but he said that Sunday was his only day to sleep in. Besides, he thought we'd have time enough to find a church once we had children. That wasn't enough for me. I really did want to go to church. I didn't know God very well, but I figured that I could know Him better if I went to church. My family hadn't been very religious, and I didn't know where to start to look for a church.

"I didn't have far to look! One morning two nice women about my age knocked on the door, said they were Bible students, and told me they would love to have a Bible study with me every week. I couldn't believe it! I didn't even have to go to church! I really looked forward to each Wednesday morning's study. I always made sure the house was cleaned early, and each week I made cookies and a pot of coffee to share with my new friends. Since I was at home alone all day, every day, it became the highlight of my week. They really cared about me.

"After several months they invited me to go with them as they went door-to-door. Then I started going to some of the meetings at the Kingdom Hall. Everyone was so friendly! And I didn't have to worry about feeling different. Everybody was studying the same books, and so our conversations were usually about the things I was already learning. My husband still wasn't interested, but he was glad I had stopped complaining about being bored.

"Within six months I made the decision to be baptized as a Jehovah's Witness. I felt so special—I was going to become a part of Jehovah's organization! I too would take the message of His Kingdom to the neighborhoods of my city. All over the world, thousands of Witnesses were taking the same message to millions of homes, fulfilling Jesus' great commission! While belonging to an accepting circle of friends who believed as I did, I had the courage to denounce the world and to stand strong against such worldly things as celebrating birthdays and the grossly commercialized 'holidays' of Christmas and Easter. When others criticized me, I only felt strengthened in my loyalty to Jehovah's organization, the Watchtower.

"I sometimes met what we called 'members of Christendom' or trinitarians as I went door-to-door, but I didn't let them bother me. They just wanted to argue and accuse me of being in a cult. Sometimes I would realize that they seemed to know the Scriptures better than I did, and that would bother me. What if I was wrong? But in the long run

I just used those feelings to push me into studying the publications of the Watchtower Society more and more. Someday I would know enough, and if there were any questions I couldn't answer, I would turn to the brothers at the Kingdom Hall and they would be sure to have an answer."

SHATTERED WORLD

"Then, after 16 years as one of Jehovah's Christian witnesses, my world shattered. My 15-year-old son was arrested for joyriding in a stolen car. The news was all over our small town within hours. Doug was not a bad boy, but he was both headstrong and immature. He didn't like the restrictive life of the Witnesses, and he and I argued about it often. Sometimes I thought he disagreed with the Witnesses just because he knew it would make me angry. Also, in his immaturity he wanted to be accepted by his friends at school. He would do almost anything to avoid being called a sissy.

"In addition to the punishment my husband gave Doug and the probation he received from the court, the elders at the Kingdom Hall urged me to get Doug enrolled in the ministerial training school on Thursday nights and to take him door-to-door to occupy his time in Jehovah's work. It was a disaster! Many of the parents of the other kids enrolled in the Thursday night study didn't want their sons (or daughters) spending time with Doug. They said he was too worldly. Rejected by his peers among the Witnesses, Doug had nowhere to turn but his 'worldly' friends at school. As if to prove his rejection of 'God's way,' Doug began running with a wild crowd of boys at the local high school. He got into more trouble. Eventually he was sent to a boys' camp for six months.

"For the first time I didn't feel a part of my congregation anymore. The children of my 'friends' wouldn't play with my children. They were told that my children were un-disciplined and didn't love Jehovah. My Witness friends began telling me that it was my husband's fault, since he had never become a Witness. One of the elders and his wife sat down with me to discuss what they said was 'the ruination of my family by my husband's sinfulness.'

"For the first time I didn't agree. It was true that my husband had never become a Witness, but he was the best husband and father I could ever hope for, aside from that. He had a genuine love for me and the children. Although he said he didn't want to become a Witness, he had always followed the Bible's guidelines with the children and with me. In fact, he could relate to Doug better than I could! Over an eight-month period my relationship to the others in my congregation had deteriorated to the point that I was rarely spoken to and I rarely spoke to anyone else. I still did my door-to-door work, but out of habit, not out of conviction. I was at least as lonely as I had been when I was a young housewife, before I joined the Witnesses."

THE LOVE OF CLARA

"Then I met Clara Guest. I knocked on her door one morning when it was just starting to rain and I ended up staying for two hours, until the rain stopped and I could walk the length of the street to my car. I was glad that my usual partner had been sick and I had decided to go anyway. I didn't really want anyone to know how much I had enjoyed talking to a non-Witness—and a pastor's wife, at that!

"Even though Clara said she believed in the Trinity and was a confirmed Protestant, I didn't feel that she either threatened me or was afraid of me. She didn't push her doctrines on me, but she did tell me that she disagreed with me. She seemed genuinely concerned with what I believed, and she wasn't intimidating.

"Clara spent most of the time talking about how important it is for us to serve God for the right reasons, and to be sure that we are serving the God of the Bible. She said that she had first joined her church because she wanted to belong somewhere and because she wanted friends who thought the way she did. Later she realized that, if God is really there, then we should serve Him because He is our Creator and because He loves us and we love Him—not because we want something selfish out of it. She said that when she finally turned her life over to God through Jesus Christ, with no strings attached, her whole life began to change. She ultimately did feel like she belonged, and she did have lots of friends, but that was now much less important to her than knowing that God loved her and that she was pleasing Him. She also emphasized the importance of knowing, from the Bible, who God is. Many people and religious groups have ideas about God, but only the Bible tells us who He really is.

"Over the next few weeks, Clara's conversation stuck with me. I could see myself in Clara's story. I too had been hungry for companionship. I had never really, honestly, sat down to study my Bible to see who God was without my already-learned Watchtower conception of Him. I stopped going door-to-door so that I would have plenty of time to study my Bible in addition to my Watchtower book and publication studies. The world view I perceived in the Bible didn't fit what I had been taught as a Witness. The God of the Bible seemed more like the God that Clara knew. I went back to see her four more times before I stopped attending Kingdom Hall. She never pressured me, never ridiculed me, and always encouraged me to study my Bible. She let me read it for myself and come up with my own understanding of it, without any coaching from her.

"Finally, four years after my son first got into trouble, and 20 years after I became a Witness, I knew I had to leave. I knew that the God of the Watchtower was not the God of the Bible. I knew that what I wanted more than friends, acceptance, and family was a right relationship with God and the assurance that He loved me and forgave me for my sins. I wrote my letter of resignation from the Society in the morning, threw all my Watchtower publications in the trash, and went over to Clara's. I announced my decision to her and asked her to pray with me so that I could receive Jesus Christ as my personal Savior."

NEW LIFE AT LAST

"Twelve years later, I can say that I have never been sorry for my decision. My new life in Christ is happy, contented, dynamic, and most of all, unfettered. I don't care what any organization or individual thinks of me. I only care what my Lord and Savior, Jesus Christ, thinks of me.

"The changes in my life made such an impression on my husband that two years after I was born again, he accepted Christ. Doug lost his resentment of religion after I left the Watchtower and he became a Christian through the witness of a friend in his office eight years ago. Now he and his wife are running a Christian home for boys who are in trouble, like he was as a teenager. Two of my other children are Christians, and we're praying for the three who are still not saved. I know now that God is just and all-knowing, and that He will give them every opportunity to come to Him. He won't judge them on the basis of organizational affiliation, but on the basis of their acceptance of His Son. I know who God is now!"

4/ ANSWERS TO THE MORMONS

Joyce and Kevin were relaxing before dinner, discussing the homework they hadn't quite finished for their Bible study later that evening. When the knock came on the door, Kevin rose to answer it. Two young men with white shirts and ties were at the door. Each held what looked like black leather Bibles.

"It's a real pleasure to be in your home, Mr. . .?" The sandy-haired young man stuck out his hand to Kevin.

Kevin reciprocated with his hand, saying, "Kevin Howard, and my wife, Joyce. Who are you?"

"As I was saying, it's a real pleasure to be in your home, Mr. Howard. We're calling from the Church of Jesus Christ of Latter-day Saints. With which church are you most familiar?"

"I'm a member of the Central Baptist Church on Garfield Avenue. Are you two Christians too? I don't think I'm familiar with your church."

The young Mormon missionaries sidestepped Kevin's question with "There are certainly a great many different

Christian churches in the world today. In your own mind, Mr. Howard, why do you think there are so many?''

"I guess because so many people interpret the Bible so differently and can't get along," Kevin answered absently as he tried to remember why the "Church of Jesus Christ of Latter-day Saints" sounded so familiar.

The missionary answered, "I'm sure that's part of it. Back in ancient times, when there were living prophets upon the earth, how did the Lord give men the answers to questions like this?''

Kevin half-smiled at the easy questions. This was easier than Bible study! "God spoke through His prophets. You could count on the answer being from God. They spoke for God.''

The second missionary, Elder Tanner, responded, "Yes, they did. I'm sure you've wondered what it was like to live back in the time of the prophets. Suppose you had lived then. You could have gone to a living prophet for an answer from God. Even today, how could a living prophet help us to find the true church?''

"That's easy," responded Kevin, "he could tell us God's opinion for sure.''

Elder Tanner smiled, "You're right. As you think about the confusion among the churches, you can see one of the needs for a living prophet today: to teach us the truth about religion.''

The sandy-haired elder, Elder Jones, picked up from Elder Tanner: "Mr. Howard, the reason we have gathered together here today is to tell you about a prophet called by the Lord in our own time. His name was Joseph Smith. He wanted to join a church, but as he visited those in his neighborhood he found this same confusion about which we have been talking. So he decided to pray and ask God which of the churches was right. As he was praying he saw a pillar of light exactly over his head. When the light rested upon him he saw, standing above him in the air, God and Jesus Christ. They spoke with him and told him what true Christianity is all about. His teachings are so important because they come from Joseph Smith's direct contacts with God. He is the prophet for today. May we come in and share more with you?''

Now Kevin remembered who they were—the Mormons! His Sunday school teacher had said something negative about them. They seemed nice enough, but Kevin wasn't taking any chances. "We really don't have time to talk with you now, Elder Jones. We're getting ready to eat dinner and then we have to go to our Bible study. But give me your phone number and I'll call you if we can get together some other time.''

Elder Jones quickly held out a piece of paper, saying, "Just give us *your* phone number, Mr. Howard, and we'll call you back in a few days. We would really like to study God's Word with you soon.''

As Kevin shut the door he turned to Joyce. "Let's ask Mr. Hicks at Sunday school about them, Joyce. I think they believe some strange things. They might even be a cult. Let's find out before we talk to them again.''

THE LATTER-DAY SAINTS

Over four million people trust the Church of Jesus Christ of Latter-day Saints (Mormon) with their salvation. These people are members of a church which claims to be the restoration of Christianity on earth today, proclaimed by God through the prophet Joseph Smith and his successors. Over four million people are taught that there are many gods, that our God was once a man like us, that we may progress to godhood ourselves, and that all non-Mormon religions and churches are an abomination to God. These four-million-plus people support the Mormon Church with their tithes and offerings, supporting a monolithic economic structure counted as one of the top 50 corporations in the country.

Mormon Church holdings include the Bonneville International Corporation, the Beneficial Life Insurance Company, the Elberta Farm Corporation, the Hawaiian Polynesian Cultural Center, and the Management Systems Corporation. The Church invests in many corporate enterprises, including 28 million dollars' worth of stock in the Times Mirror Corporation, publishers of the *Los Angeles Times*. Two of the Mormon Church's largest contributors are J. Willard Marriott (billionaire hotel and restaurant owner) and the Osmond Family of entertainers.[1] The economic and spiritual power of the Mormon Church is immense and presents a strong challenge to the historic Christian faith.

Historically, Mormonism has been considered a cult because its primary teachings are completely opposed to the cardinal teachings of the Bible, reflected in Christian church history. Rather than obeying the Bible as the final and absolute guide for all truth, Mormonism teaches that the Bible is insufficient and contains mistakes. To the Bible is added *The Book of Mormon, The Pearl of Great Price, Doctrine and Covenants,* and the words of the president of the church. Ezra Taft Benson, the man who will one day be president of the Mormon Church (to be elected upon the death of current president Spencer W. Kimball), declared in 1980 that "the prophet can never lead the church astray because he receives direct revelations from God." He even maintained that the words of the current president are more important than any past revelations, including the Bible and the other standard Mormon works.[2] By departing from obedience to the Bible, the Mormon Church has prepared the way for further doctrinal deviation, which confirms its standing outside the body of Christ, the Christian church. Shortly we will discuss the other doctrinal deviations of the Mormon Church concerning its beliefs about God, Jesus Christ, mankind, sin, and salvation.

WHO BECOMES A MORMON?

As we discussed in the opening chapters, while several different kinds of people are attracted to cults, certain characteristics seem to predispose someone to being attracted to a cult. The cornerstone of a Mormon's faith is based on his personal "testimony." Unlike normal Christian testimonies, the Mormon testimony is a "burning in the bosom," an emotional experience that follows "sincere prayer" about the authenticity of *The Book of Mormon*. A Mormon is not likely to examine his faith rationally because he did not acquire his faith rationally. His spiritual life is governed by his emotions, and he finds it difficult to test spiritual teachings, as we are instructed in 1 Thessalonians 5:21,22: "Test everything. Hold on to the good. Avoid every kind of evil." Since the Mormon has been taught that testimonies are very important, we as Christians can use our testimonies, based on rational faith in the Word of God, to effectively present the gospel to Mormons.

When we discuss the Mormon belief about God, we will see that the Mormon God (of this earth) is a simple god, one easy to understand, one like man, attractive to the person who doesn't like a complex God beyond his complete comprehension but who instead desires a God who is small enough to figure out completely. The Mormon God is big enough to be an authority figure, big enough to direct one's spiritual life, but not big enough to challenge a man's basic egocentricity. The Mormon at your door is sincerely obedient to the truth he sees in the Mormon Church, while at the same time confident that, with the help of his church, he can comprehend the mysteries of God that the traditional church has declared beyond the ability of human finiteness to completely comprehend.

Even when a Mormon discovers that the Mormon Church is a counterfeit of the real church of God, he may be reluctant to leave the security of the church that has provided him with every spiritual, social, and emotional need (even if inadequately) during his membership. Because of the strong emphasis on the loyalty of the family to the Mormon Church, a Mormon contemplating leaving the church is in real danger of dividing his family and even of being an outcast to his own family.

Most Mormon missionaries are young men who come from Mormon families. The ones at your door may feel that they have nowhere else to go if they leave the Mormon Church. The gospel you share with them may appear to be a gospel devoid of family, security, and self-worth. The Mormon missionary is looked up to by the congregation (stake) he serves. He may not want to leave such a position of importance for what appears, from the outside, to be a lowly position of just-converted novice Christian. When we share our faith with Mormons, we have the opportunity to share our intimate relationship with Christ and our unique standing as a chosen child of God. The Mormon who is willing to risk everything for genuine peace with God through the intercession of Christ our Lord loses nothing by comparison to what he receives in Christ. Jesus reminds us, "Anyone who loves his father or mother more than me is not worthy of me . . . and anyone who does not take his cross and follow me is not worthy of me. Whoever finds his life will lose it, and whoever loses his life for my sake will find it" (Matthew 10:37-39).

CHANGING THE MEANINGS

Before we look at Mormon history and at what Mormonism teaches about God, Jesus Christ, mankind, sin, salvation, and the Bible, we need to remind ourselves of the fact that the cults, including Mormonism, take the vocabulary of the Bible and redefine it to fit their own views.

Semantics is the study of words—how they are used and how their meanings have developed. This includes the different definitions and uses by different people of the same words. By understanding the semantics of Mormon theology, we can see clearly the differences between Mormonism and Christianity. So remember that Mormonism takes words like God, Jesus Christ, the Holy Ghost, and the Trinity and gives them meanings foreign to the Bible.

We will find out that to the Mormon, "God" refers to a belief in many gods, none of whom are eternal, and one of whom is the ruler over this planet. The Jesus Christ of Mormonism is Lucifer's brother, the earthly product of sexual relations between God and Mary. Mormonism's Holy Ghost is a god separate from the Father and the Son, the only god in Mormonism's "trinity" without a material body. The Trinity of Mormonism is not one God in three Persons, as the Bible reveals, but three separate gods, each of whom has had dealings with our planet. If we keep this semantical puzzle in mind when we turn to the beliefs of Mormonism, the differences between Mormonism and Christianity will be clear.

MORMON BEGINNINGS

The Mormon Church was founded on April 6, 1830, near Palmyra, New York by Joseph Smith and a few of his closest friends. It has grown in membership from the original six members to over four million members. Though plagued by dissension and persecution in its early years, the church has seen steady growth through all of this century and spectacular growth for the last 20 years.

Founder and "prophet" Joseph Smith, Jr., was born in Sharon, Vermont, in 1805 but lived in Palmyra, near Rochester, New York, by the time he claimed his religious visions at age 15. His family was poor and not well-respected in the community. In his later autobiography (contained in *The Pearl of Great Price* as "The History of Joseph Smith the Prophet"), Smith claimed that, as he was praying for divine guidance concerning which religion to join, God the Father and Jesus Christ appeared to him. He asked them which sect he should join, and, in his own words, "I was answered that I must join none of them for they were all wrong; and the Personage who addressed me said . . .'they draw near to me with their lips, but their hearts are far from me; they teach for doctrines the commandments of men, having a form of godliness, but they deny the power thereof.' He again forbade me to join with any of them; and many other things did he say unto me, which I cannot write at this time."[3] This is the Mormon Church's claim to divine origin.

In subsequent years further revelations called Smith to be the leader of God's restoration of Christianity upon the earth and to be the inspired translator of a new Bible, the "Golden Bible," written on golden plates which has been buried under a hill (Cumorrah) near Palmyra. This book is now known as *The Book of Mormon*. By 1830 the book was translated and published, and the Church of Jesus Christ of Latter-day Saints was established.

During its early years the church and its members moved from New York to Kirtland, Ohio; then to Independence, Missouri; then to Nauvoo, Illinois. Smith ruled the community with a tight rein and was obeyed implicitly by all his followers as God's prophet for today. During his 14 years of leadership he "miraculously translated" the long-lost "Book of Abraham" (now part of *The Pearl of Great Price*), a papyrus he found in a mummy case which he had purchased from a traveling salesman. He wrote his own history and worked on an "Inspired Version" of the Bible. He claimed to have received a revelation from God on July 12, 1843, which stated that it was desirable to have more than one wife as a means of propagating more saints for the Mormon Church.

Widespread persecution drove the small church from Missouri back to Illinois, where an entire Mormon community, Nauvoo, was formed under Smith's direction. But even a private community was no permanent protection against the persecution of outsiders, and in June of 1844 Joseph Smith and his brother Hyrum were jailed in Carthage, Illinois. On June 27 Joseph and Hyrum were killed by angry townspeople before they could be brought to trial. The Mormon Church declared their prophet a martyr for the faith.

Brigham Young (1801-77) was elected the new president of the church, and in 1846 he led the members from Illinois to the "promised land," Salt Lake Basin, in the Utah territory. The husband of many wives, the father of many children, and the leader of a social, material, and economic empire, Brigham Young died in 1877, having transformed the Mormon Church from a small band of poor farmers to a powerful coalition of thousands of people.

Under United States government pressure, the President of the church, Wilford Woodruff in 1890 received a revelation stating that polygamy was only to be enjoyed in the celestial kingdom (heaven). This was the most important change in

Mormon belief until 1978, when President Kimball received a purported revelation ending 150 years of Mormon discrimination against Blacks.[4]

The Mormon Church today is a vast religious, social, and economic empire ruled by the General Authorities of the Church of Jesus Christ of Latter-day Saints, consisting of the First Presidency, the Council of the Twelve, the Partriarch to the Church, the Presidency of the First Quorum of the Seventy, the First Quorum of the Seventy, and the Presiding Bishopric. Secret temple rites are performed in the 20 temples scattered around the world (the newest being in Japan and Seattle). Mormon missionaries, who volunteer two years of their lives (usually between high school and college) to proselytize for the church, are full of zeal as they pedal their bicycles from door to door. What kind of gospel do they bring to our doors, and how can we give them solid answers from the Word of God?

MORMON TEACHINGS

Religious Books

The Mormon standard works include *The Book of Mormon, The Pearl of Great Price, Doctrine and Covenants,* and the Bible. These four works are claimed as the sources for Mormon teaching, along with continuing revelation by the President.

The Book of Mormon claims to be a history of the American Indians, who descended from Jews, who migrated from the Mideast to South America centuries ago. Jesus Christ visited them and proclaimed the gospel to them. The history was hidden centuries ago by Mormon, a faithful Nephite prophet, under a hill in upstate New York. Although the true origin of *The Book of Mormon* may never be known positively, we can confidently state that its origin is not with the God of the Bible. Not only does *The Book of Mormon* contradict the Bible in numerous places, but it is full of archeological errors. Today's version has more than 3900 changes from the 1830 edition of "the most correct of any book on earth," which was probably an adulterated form of a historical novel written before 1816 by Rev. Samuel Spalding.[5]

The Pearl of Great Price is a one-volume collection of shorter works, including Joseph Smith's history, *The Book of Abraham*, a portion of Joseph Smith's Bible "translation," and the Mormon Articles of Faith.

The History of Joseph Smith the Prophet

This section of *The Pearl of Great Price* is completely at variance with the known history of Joseph Smith and the Mormon Church. Historical research establishes the earliest date of Smith's first claimed vision at late 1824, while *The Pearl of Great Price* claims that it was in 1820 and that his second vision was in 1823. Smith's family was not well-respected or liked in the community of Palmyra, as a number of witnesses of the time attested. Nor was Joseph Smith himself well-liked or respected. A contemporary described him:

> Joe was the most ragged, lazy fellow in the place, and that is saying a good deal. He was about 25 years old. I can see him now, in my mind's eye, with his torn and patched trousers held to his form by a pair of suspenders made out of sheeting, with his calico shirt as dirty and black as the earth, and his uncombed hair sticking through the holes in his old battered hat. . . . He was known among the young men I associated with as a

romancer of the first water. I never knew so ignorant a man as Joe was to have such a fertile imagination.[6]
There are numerous other discrepancies between the history in *The Pearl of Great Price* and objective historical investigation.

The Book of Abraham

This section purports to be a translated narrative from Abraham. The Egyptian papyrus from which it was "translated," along with Smith's translation notes on the backs of the sheets, were lost and presumed destroyed. However, they have now been found and the Mormon Church has verified their authenticity. Translation by reputable translators reveals, instead of a message from Abraham, Egyptian funerary verses! This section also contains the infamous indictment of blacks, which was the basis for years of discrimination by the Mormon Church, until the purported revelation of 1978.

The Mormon Articles of Faith

The Mormon presupposition against the Bible as the only standard for truth is evident in these articles, which declare that the Bible is correct only insofar as it is correctly translated, while *The Book of Mormon* is God's Word without reservation.

Doctrine and Covenants

This part of Mormon scripture is a collection of revelations given to Joseph Smith which deal primarily with Mormon teachings and practices. First published as *The Book of Com-*

mandments, they were added to, changed, and reprinted in 1835 as *Doctrine and Covenants*. There are at least 65,000 changes between the first and the present edition of the work.[7]

Doctrine and Covenants contains both God's establishment of polygamy as an everlasting covenant and His revocation of that same covenant in 1890 by Mormon President Wilford Woodruff! *The Book of Mormon* condemns polygamy (Jacob 2:24) and the Bible condemns polygamy (Deuteronomy 17:17; 1 Timothy 3:2,12; Titus 1:6; Matthew 19:4-6).

The Mormon position on Scripture is completely opposed to the historic Christian position: that the Bible, and the Bible alone, is the infallible and inerrant guide to God's truth.

Your answer to the Mormon at your door who agrees that he accepts "scripture" as God's Word, but means by this the Mormon standard works, is to share with him the reasonableness and consistency of our God. The God of the Bible does not contradict Himself, and the Old and New Testaments are accurate reflections of His message to man. We can be confident of the contents of His original revelations through the work of scholars in the fields of language, literature, textual criticism, history, and archeology.[8] Jesus Christ claimed divine origin for the Old and New Testaments (Luke 24:25-27; John 15:26, 27; 16:12-15). Any continuing revelations from God cannot contradict what God has already said. Can the Mormon trust his eternal life to a God who is fickle and inconsistent? The Christian has the promise that his God "does not change like shifting shadows. He chose to give us birth through the word of truth, that we might be a kind of firstfruits of all he created" (James 1:17,18).

MORMON DOCTRINES

The Mormon God

We will briefly present and then Biblically refute the Mormon ideas about God, including polytheism (belief in more than one god), an unscriptural Trinity, an unbiblical Jesus, the erroneous idea that Adam is our God, and progression to godhood.

Polytheism is the belief in more than one true God, even if no more than one god is worshiped. Joseph Smith asserted the existence of more than one God in his *History of the Church* (6:305-306): "You have got to learn how to be gods yourselves, and to be kings and priests to God, the same as all gods have done before you. . . ." We could properly say that Mormons are *henotheistic,* a form of polytheism which means that you worship one god out of the many gods in existence.

As Christians who believe the Bible, we are *monotheists,* meaning that we believe in the existence of only one true God and that we worship only this one true God, who is revealed to us in the Bible as the Father, the Son, and the Holy Spirit. First Corinthians 8:4-6 explains that there are created things which men may call gods, but to us to whom God has spoken, there is only one true God. Deuteronomy 6:4, the Hebrew affirmation of faith, declares, "Hear, O Israel: The Lord our God, the Lord is one." Quite clearly, Isaiah 43:10 explains that there is only one God from all eternity: " 'You are my witnesses,' declares the Lord, 'and my servant whom I have chosen, so that you may know and believe me and understand that I am he. Before me no god was formed, nor will there be one after me.' " Although the Bible only has to affirm something once for it to be true, the Bible *repeatedly* affirms that there is only one true God (see, among many passages, Isaiah 44:6-8; 1 Timothy 2:5; John 17:3).

The Mormon Trinity

The Mormon trinity is not the Trinity of the historic Christian church, the Trinity as revealed in the Bible. The Mormon trinity is a triad of three gods in cooperation with each other. The Mormon Father God has a body "as tangible as man's." The Mormon Jesus has also "earned" a body on this earth, while the Holy Ghost is a god without a tangible body. Mormonism declares, "The Father has a body of flesh and bone as tangible as man's; the Son also; but the Holy Ghost has not a body of flesh and bones, but is a personage of spirit."⁹ Joseph Smith even said, "These three constitute three distinct personages and three Gods."¹⁰

As we have already seen, the Bible flatly denies the existence of more than one true God. When we say that we believe in the Trinity, we do not believe, as the Mormons do, in three gods, or, as the Jehovah's Witnesses say we do, in a strange "three-headed" god. We believe, simply, that within the one nature of the one changeless personal God eternally exist three divine Persons: the Father, the Son, and the Holy Spirit (Ghost). We have already discussed some of the verses (as Isaiah 43:10) that show that there is only one true God. Second Peter 1:17 tells us that the Father is God; John 1:1,14 tells us that the Son is God; Acts 5:3,4 tells us that the Holy Spirit is God. We do not believe in one God in three Gods, or in one Person in three Persons. God is not one-in-three and three-in-one in the same sense. He is *one God in three divine Persons* (see Matthew 28:19; Genesis 1:26; Isaiah 6:3,8; 48:16; Luke 3:22; John 14:16).¹¹

There have been false ideas of the Trinity for centuries—almost since the time of the apostles. Most unbiblical ideas concerning the Trinity can be grouped under either *Arianism, Subordinationism,* or *Modalism.* Arianism makes only the Father God and reduces the Son (and usually the Holy Spirit) to demigod or created status. Subordinationism, like Mormonism, believes in more than one God, with one of the three Gods, usually the Father, being the ruling God. Modalism blurs the distinction among the Persons of the Godhead, confusing the Father with the Son and Spirit, and vice versa.

The Mormon Jesus

To the Mormons, Jesus is a completely separate god from the Father, who is called Elohim or Michael or Adam. The Mormon Jesus is also called Jehovah, although he is not eternally God, as the name Jehovah (from I AM) implies. Instead, Jesus was the spirit-brother of Lucifer (*The Doctrinal Commentary on the Pearl of Great Price,* pp. 107-109). Jesus was not begotten by the Holy Spirit but was the product of sexual union between Mary and God (Adam or Our Father). Brigham Young declared:

Now remember from this time forth, and forever, that Jesus Christ was not begotten by the Holy Ghost.[12]

The Mormon view of Jesus Christ directly opposes the Bible. Jesus is the unique Son of God, not the spirit-brother of Lucifer. John 1:14 declares, "The Word became flesh and lived for a while among us. We have seen his glory, the glory of the one and only Son, who came from the Father, full of grace and truth." Two of the four Gospels clearly attest to the virgin birth and conception of Jesus. In contrast to Brigham Young, Matthew 1:18-20 states:

This is how the birth of Jesus Christ came about. His mother Mary was pledged to be married to Joseph, but before they came together, she was found to be with child through the Holy Spirit. Because Joseph her husband was a righteous man and did not want to expose her to public disgrace, he had in mind to divorce her quietly.

But after he had considered this, an angel of the Lord appeared to him in a dream and said, "Joseph son of David, do not be afraid to take Mary home as your wife, because what is conceived in her is from the Holy Spirit" (See also Luke 1:34,35).

The Father is not an exalted man-god who physically impregnated Mary. John 4:24, Isaiah 31:3; and Numbers 23:19 make it clear that God is immaterial. (When Mormons point to Bible verses describing, for example, God's "arms," "feet," "eyes," etc., we should remember that the infinite God, when described to us finite people, must be described in our finite language. Such description is metaphorical and figurative.)

The Mormon Adam-God

Mormon writings are confusing in regard to the identity of their Father God. During at least a portion of Mormon history, God "revealed" through Prophet Brigham Young that the Adam of the Garden of Eden is "our Father and our God."[13] However, a later Mormon Prophet, Joseph Fielding Smith, identified Elohim as the first god of the Trinity, our Father, and that Adam is a different god, Michael the Archangel, who helped to organize the earth. Today's Mormons generally deny that Adam is our God. It may not be possible to determine authoritative Mormon identification of its gods, but we can see that such identification is at best confused and contradictory. The God of the Bible, on the other hand, is not confusing and contradictory. While full comprehension of His infinite Being is impossible for us who are finite, what He has revealed to us is constant and noncontradictory (James 1:17).

The Mormon Progression to Godhood

The Mormon concept of God is not the Biblical concept of God. Mormonism teaches that there is an infinite *regression* of gods in the past and an infinite *progression* of gods (beings becoming gods and growing in their deity) in the future.

Mormonism teaches that there were eternally existing spirit beings called intelligences (*Gospel through the Ages,* pp. 126-29) who were then clothed with spirit bodies, begotten and born by heavenly parents, and raised to maturity as spirit sons and daughters. These spirit sons and daughters are then born of physical parents on earth, receive physical bodies, and go through "mortality." Once they have died, they are assigned, on the basis of their good works on earth and as spirits earlier in heaven, to one of three levels in heaven. The highest level is the celestial level, and those who get there become gods. Even the supreme Mormon God got to be a god by this same progression, which goes on eternally with an infinite number of "spirits." James Talmadge, in *Articles of Faith* (p. 430), affirmed:

> We believe in a God who is Himself progressive . . . whose perfection consists in eternal advancement—a Being who has attained His exalted state by a path which now His children are permitted to follow, whose glory it is their heritage to share.

We cannot accept the Mormon progression of godhood on either logical or Biblical grounds.

There cannot logically be an eternal regression or progression of finite gods. In the final analysis, such a system does not provide us with sufficient cause for the existence of anything. While it may be convenient to say, "It just has always happened that way and will always happen that way," such thinking is irrational. The Mormon falls into the trap of the agnostic, who always queries, "If God made everything, then who made God?" The Mormon has no rational answer: he must reply that another god made this god, and another god made that god, and another god made that god, and so on, without ever answering the question satisfactorily at all.

As Bible-believing Christians, we answer that no one made God: He is not made at all, but is eternal, without beginning, without progression, and without ending. The Bible defines God as the uncreated, eternal Being whose existence is necessary as the ultimate cause of all other beings. By such a definition the agnostic is answered, "No one made God. By definition He is the uncreated Cause of everything else. As the Bible puts it, he is the Beginning and the End (Revelation 21:6).

The Mormon "infinite regression" is an insufficient cause for existence. By promoting an infinite regression of gods, the Mormon is merely soliciting an additional "But who made that god?" question from critics. Examples of this reasoning in more concrete terms can show the futility of infinite regression or progression. Suppose you want permission to borrow a calculator. You ask your supervisor. Your supervisor asks his supervisor. His supervisor asks his supervisor. His supervisor asks his supervisor, and so on forever. Do you ever receive permission to borrow the calculator? No, because for you to receive the calculator, someone somewhere must have the independent authority to lend you the calculator. Infinite regression accomplishes nothing.

Another example will clarify the futility of infinite progression. Suppose you ask me the definition of the word "gorp." I tell you it means "smyt." You ask what "smyt" means. I tell you it means "wog." You ask what "wog" means. I tell you it means "borl," etc. Do you ever find out what "gorp" means? No matter how long the vocabulary list gets, even infinitely long, unless you come to a word you already know, you will never find out what "gorp" really means. Infinite progression accomplishes nothing.

The true Biblical God is also against Mormonism's regressional and progressional gods. The Biblical God is eternally perfect, never changing or progressing. We have already discussed Isaiah 43;10, 11. Malachi 3:6 quotes God as saying: "I the Lord do not change." Revelation 1:8 expresses His eternal nature: " 'I am the Alpha and the Omega,' says the Lord God, who is and who was and who is to come, the Almighty."

We have seen that the Mormon God (gods) is incompatible with the Biblical God and with the logic that God has given us. Scripture denies the validity of Mormonism's deity. When the Mormons at your door try to say that they believe in the same God you do, you can show them from the Bible the God we believe in as Christians. Point out to them that only the Biblical God is a sufficient and necessary cause of all creation. Point out to them that our God is not growing and changing, but is eternally complete and perfect. After they understand the Biblical concept of God, you can show them how they can come into a right relationship with that God through the salvation offered by Jesus Christ and declared to us in the Bible. You can then assure the Mormons that they too can join the "priesthood of all believers" and enjoy a personal relationship with the true God of the universe.

The Mormon Salvation

In Mormonism there are two kinds of salvation. Hardly anyone goes to "hell," according to Mormon theology. Instead, there is a general salvation, equivalent to resurrection, which almost everyone attains. This "salvation" is for those who have died in ignorance of the "restored gospel," or Mormonism. The second kind of Mormon salvation is personal and is only for those who fulfill the "ordinances of the gospel." This is also known as "exaltation." There are eight main requirements for exaltation: faith, repentance, baptism, laying on of hands, church membership, keeping the commandments, accepting Joseph Smith and his successors as God's mouthpiece, and temple works.[14]

Mormon salvation fits into the pattern of the eternal progression that we have already discussed. In this eternal progression, those who die after their human existence can attain one of three degrees of glory: the telestial glory, where unbelievers go; the terrestrial glory, where good, sincere, religious non-Mormons go; and the celestial glory, where only obedient Mormons go and where godhood is attained. Mormons misinterpret 1 Corinthians 15:40,41 and 2 Corinthians 12:1-4 to try to support this theory.

The Bible teaches only one kind of salvation, available to all people on the same basis of faith and grace: salvation through the Son of God, Jesus Christ, whose sacrifice is sufficient to cover all our sins. First Corinthians 15:40,41 does not discuss degrees of heaven; it discusses by metaphor the difference between our corruptible bodies and our resurrection bodies. Second Corinthians 12:1-4 does not teach that there are three levels to the dwelling place of God (heaven); it uses the common descriptive means of its day to distinguish among the air we breathe (the first heaven), the vault of stars, moon, and planets (the second heaven), and the dwelling place of God (the third heaven).

The Bible tells us that there is only one action required to gain eternal salvation: believing in the Lord Jesus Christ (Acts 16:30,31). Our exaltation in God's sight is accomplished the moment we trust Jesus Christ for our salvation. It does not depend at all on our works, but only on Christ's work for us on the cross. When Jesus was asked what works men could do to be saved, He responded, "The work of God is this: to believe in the one he has sent" (John 6:28,29). Because He is the unique Son of God, the God-man, "he is able to save completely those who come to God through him, because he always lives to intercede for them" (Hebrews 7:25). Paul summarized the all-encompassing salvation work of Christ in Romans 5:8-11:

> But God demonstrates his own love for us in this: While we were still sinners, Christ died for us.
>
> Since we have now been justified by his blood, how much more shall we be saved from God's wrath through him! For if, when we were God's enemies, we were reconciled to him through the death of his Son, how much more, having been reconciled, shall we be saved through his life! Not only is this so, but we also rejoice in God through our Lord Jesus Christ, through whom we have now received reconciliation.

Our works do not play any part at all in our salvation; instead, they *demonstrate* our salvation to other people, as declared in Romans 4:1-8 and James 2:14-26. (James 2 is a favorite passage which the Mormons use to try to prove that salvation is by works. But when we compare this passage with its counterpart in Romans 6, we see that works are the *evidence* of true salvation rather than the cause of it.) Ephesians 2:8-10 declares:

For it is by grace you have been saved, through
faith—and this is not from yourselves, it is the gift of
God—not by works, so that no one can boast. For we are
God's workmanship, created in Christ Jesus to do good
works, which God prepared in advance for us to do.

We can be sure of our eternal communion with God because
of the Bible's promise that "he who began a good work in you
will carry it on to completion until the day of Christ Jesus"
(Philippians 1:6).

The Mormon Authority

It is sometimes difficult to express Biblical truths to the
Mormons at your door because of their concept of divine
authority, which to them resides exclusively in the Mormon
Church's two priesthoods. Because the Mormons at your door
"have the priesthood" and you do not, they do not believe
that your beliefs have any validity. By understanding the basics
of the Mormon priesthood system in contrast to the Biblical
position of the authority of the believer, you can learn to communicate effectively with the Mormons at your door.

Mormons believe that all religious or God-given authority
resides in the Mormon Church, which is organized with prophets, apostles, and priests. These Mormon teachings on authority are based on the Mormon belief that the entire church
apostatized, or left the truth, shortly after the apostolic age.
Because of this apostasy, a "restoration" is necessary in the
form of the Mormon Church. They misinterpret such Bible
verses as Acts 20:29,30 (which does not teach total apostasy,
but which warns us to guard the apostolic truths of the gospel,
as was done by faithful believers throughout all ages); 2
Thessalonians 2:3 (which also does not teach total apostasy,
but a partial apostasy at the end of the age, when the man of
lawlessness is revealed, and that such an apostasy will deceive

"those who are perishing . . . because they refused to love the truth and so be saved—verse 10); and 1 Timothy 4:1-3 (which clearly states that *some* will abandon the faith, not all). Even *The Book of Mormon* denies a *total* apostasy, since it claims that four "apostles" remained alive with the truth of the gospel (III Nephi 28;cf. *Doctrine and Covenants* 7).

Mormons try to use Ephesians 2:20 to support their hierarchy of apostles and prophets. However, the verse is speaking of the *foundation* of the church, of which we need only *one* (not a new one each generation). Just as a building needs only one foundation, so Paul says the church has only one foundation. According to the New Testament, those who were apostles must have seen the risen Lord (1 Corinthians 15:1-8), must have been personally called by Christ (Galatians 1:1,11,12,16,19), and must have been taught the gospel by Christ (Galatians 1:12). These qualifications were met by the New Testament apostles but have not been met by anyone today. In addition, Mormon apostles are voted into office by the church membership, while the New Testament apostles were chosen by Christ, regardless of man's opinion (Galatians 1:1).

Luke 16:16 and Hebrews 1:1,2 refute the Mormon claim that the church must have prophets in order to know God's will. Hebrews 1:1,2 declares:

In the past God spoke to our forefathers through the prophets at many times and in various ways, but in these last days he has spoken to us by his Son, whom he appointed heir of all things, and through whom he made the universe.

Any prophet of God, or any person claiming to speak for God, must fulfill the requirements of a prophet as outlined in Deuteronomy 13:1-5 and 18:20-22. What he says must come to pass, and he must preach the true God of the Bible. Since the Mormon prophets have taught false doctrine concerning God (including polytheism) and have made false prophecies (see, for example, *Doctrine and Covenants* 111:1-11, where Joseph Smith said that God told him that Salem, Massachusetts, would turn all its wealth over to him), they are not prophets of God but are false prophets. The Bible warns us not to follow them (Deuteronomy 13:1-4).

As we mentioned before, there are two Mormon priesthoods: the Aaronic, or lesser priesthood, and the Melchizedek, or greater priesthood. The Aaronic priesthood can be held by all obedient Mormon males from age 12, while the Melchizedek priesthood can be held only by obedient Mormon men from age 18.

The Bible, however, declares that the Aaronic priesthood was superseded by Christ's atonement and priesthood. Hebrews 5:1 through 10:21 shows how the Old Testament's priestly duties were only a shadow of Christ, our Great High Priest. Hebrews 7:11-28 makes it clear that the Aaronic, or Levitical, priesthood is completely useless now that we have Jesus, whose priesthood is like that of Melchizedek. There are not *many* priests of the line of Melchizedek, but only *one*: Jesus (see Hebrews 9:11-21). The Book of Hebrews reminds us that, while there used to be many priests, now there is only one: "Because Jesus lives forever, he has a permanent priesthood. Therefore he is able to save completely those who come to God through him, because he always lives to intercede for them. Such a high priest meets our need—one who is holy, blameless, pure, set apart from sinners, exalted above the heavens" (Hebrews 7:24-26).

While the office of priest in offering the once-for-all sacrifice for sin belongs only to Jesus, the freewill offering of ourselves as "living sacrifices" to God (Romans 12:1) gives all believers a kind of priesthood. Our authority as believers is described in John 1:12: we have "the right to become children of God." First Peter 2:5 calls us priests: "You also, like living stones, are being built into a spiritual house to be a holy priesthood, offering spiritual sacrifices acceptable to God through Jesus Christ." This same theme is reiterated in Revelation 1:5,6, where our Ruler, Jesus Christ, has made us worthy to be priests:

> . . . and from Jesus Christ, who is the faithful witness, the firstborn from the dead, and the ruler of the kings of the earth. To him who loves us and has freed us from our sins by his blood, and has made us to be a kingdom and priests to serve his God and Father—to him be glory and power for ever and ever! Amen.

Church authority is given by God for the governing of the congregations for the body of Christ, and not as a means of depositing all spiritual wisdom and Scriptural knowledge in the hands of a few people. We are saved by our relationship to Christ, not by our relationship to any organization. Although we may have different functions within the body of Christ (1 Corinthians 12:4-11), we each stand before God on the same basis: "For we were all baptized by one Spirit into one body—whether Jews or Greeks, slave or free—and we were all given the one Spirit to drink" (v. 13). Galatians 3:26-29 agrees, saying:

> You are all sons of God through faith in Christ Jesus, for all of you who were baptized into Christ have been clothed with Christ. There is neither Jew nor Greek, slave nor free, male nor female, for you are all one in Christ Jesus. If you belong to Christ, then you are Abraham's seed, and heirs according to the promise.

ANSWERS TO THE MORMONS

Although the Mormons at your door present themselves as teaching in harmony with the Bible, we have seen that Mormonism contradicts the Bible on all the essential doctrines of the Christian faith. Your witness should center around the differences between a Mormon's relationship to God and a Christian's relationship to God. Remember to keep the Person and work of Jesus Christ central to your discussion. Avoid peripheral areas of teaching. The validity of polygamy is insignificant when compared with a person's eternal destiny.

What are some differences between a Mormon's relationship to his god and a Christian's relationship to the Biblical God?

1. The Biblical God is eternal, unchanging, perfect, and complete. We need not worry that God will change His own attitudes or His requirements for us when He "matures more" tomorrow. Our God is rational and reasonable, and He has endowed us with a mind by which we are to test what other people tell us.

2. The Biblical Jesus is unique, the only Son of God, incarnated miraculously and born of a virgin. He is one in nature and essence with the Father and the Holy Ghost. Without help from us, He has perfected our salvation for all time through His sacrifice for our sins on the cross.

3. The Biblical salvation is not dependent on our own sinful and inept works, but upon God alone. He is our Savior, and there is no other. We do not have to worry about perfectly fulfilling all parts of the eight Mormon doctrines of salvation. We need only be accepted by Christ, the only One who ever perfectly fulfilled all points of the law. Our salvation rests in Him. We can know right now that we are accepted fully and freely by God through Jesus Christ our Lord.

4. The Biblical faith is not based on a complicated and contradictory organizational system administered by false prophets. Our faith is of God (Jesus Christ). We don't have to change our beliefs against all reason and every change of the Mormon presidency. Far from being part of the great apostasy, we can confidently proclaim that our faith is the faith of the apostles and prophets of old, the faith given us by

the Father, provided for by the sacrifice of the Son, and sanctified by the power of the Holy Spirit.

When you share these differences with the Mormons at your
door, you will have shared with him the gospel, the offer of
new birth "into a living hope through the resurrection of Jesus
Christ from the dead, and into an inheritance that can never
perish, spoil or fade—kept in heaven for you, who through
faith are shielded by God's power until the coming of the
salvation that is ready to be revealed in the last time"
(1 Peter 1:3-5).

HOWARD AND JUDY

Howard Nesbitt and his wife, Judy, had stopped by our
office to pick up some research on Mormonism. A young man
of about 25, Howard was getting ready to see his parents, who
were Mormons, and he wanted to be sure that he could show
them what he had learned about some of the problems of
Mormon history.

Howard came from a Mormon family. In fact, his mother's
side of the family traced its Mormon roots back to Brigham
Young's family in Utah. Howard was the only non-Mormon
in his immediate family. During the first two years after he left
the Mormon Church his family refused to even talk to him,
but in the last year they had talked twice by phone and had
now arranged a short visit.

Howard's wife, Judy, was not a Mormon when she had met
Howard in high school, but she became one shortly before
they were married. She felt that it was important for her to
agree with her new husband on religious matters, and so she
turned deaf ears to her parents, who tried to tell her she was
joining a cult. Ironically, it was Judy's parents who finally got
through to Howard and Judy and convinced them to examine
the Mormon claims, compare them to the Bible, and decide

their religious beliefs rationally. Howard and Judy shared with us the reasons they felt that this upcoming visit by Howard's parents was so important.

Howard began, "You have to understand how important the family is in the Mormon Church. Everything is centered around the family. In fact, the whole ward is like one big family. We do everything together, and our allegiance to the church is just about supreme. In our case, since our family membership went back so many generations, sticking together meant even more. If you are a Mormon in good standing, the church will take care of anything you ever need. There are activities for all the different age groups, services and meetings all week, family-home-evening once a week, and special programs that promote unity both within the family and within the church. When I first started dating Judy, my parents were completely against her. They were sure that she was going to take away my faith. They tried to tell me that I was destroying family unity and denying my faith by dating a non-Mormon. Then, when we got engaged, my father really hit the roof!"

Judy interrupted, "You see, after we first started dating, right out of high school, Howard decided to go on his mission. Most of Howard's Mormon friends went at the same time. It's really expected of Mormons in good standing to devote two years of their lives to mission work for the church. Most Mormon boys do their missions right after they get out of high school. I didn't see Howard for two whole years while he was on his mission, and I guess his parents thought it was a good way to break us up. They had no idea he would see me when he got home.

"What actually happened was that the two-year separation had given us both time to discover that our feelings were really deep. Howard called me the first day he got home, we dated the next day, and he proposed within the week. We told his parents just two weeks after he got home. It was really a shock to them. That's when Howard's dad hit the roof. He was not about to have his oldest son marry an outsider. He couldn't understand how Howard could ignore the very truths he had been teaching during his mission. Finally, his parents said that they wouldn't speak to him or allow him into their house if he married a non-Mormon."

Howard continued, "That stopped me short. I was brought up believing that your family is the most important thing you have. We even believed that there would be family units in heaven. If I hadn't wanted to marry Judy so badly, I would have dropped her right there. As it was, I really put the pressure on her to be baptized into the church. I was hoping that she would become Mormon so I wouldn't have to face losing either her or my family . Even though her parents were completely against it, she gave in pretty easily and was baptized into the Mormon church two months before we were married. I guess her parents' Christian commitment kind of worked against them for a little while. Although they were as much against Judy turning Mormon as my parents were about me marrying a non-Mormon, they didn't threaten Judy. They told her that they would still love her even if she went against their wishes, and they said they would accept me as their son-in-law even though they didn't agree with us."

LIGHT AT LAST

"In the long run, though, that same love and commitment is what got us to see the light. Although they didn't constantly criticize Mormonism, they did continue to let us know that they didn't think Mormonism was Christian. When it worked naturally into the conversation, they would point out the differences between what the Bible taught and what Mormonism taught.

"For example, Judy and I became very active in our stake.

It seemed like every minute was taken up with church work. A lot of people think that Mormons believe that salvation is by works, plain and simple. Well, it's not that simple. I had a true love for God and a desire to please Him and provide for my family both here and in the next life. I was taught that my love was truly shown in what I did for the church. So, when I did all this work, I wasn't doing it because of a selfish save-my-own-skin motive, but because I really thought that this was to please God and provide for my family. But I didn't know where to stop. I didn't know how much was enough to please God and protect my family. God didn't talk to me. All I had to go on was the teachings of the church. God spoke to the whole church through our scriptures, our prophet (the president of the church), and our church leaders. But He wouldn't speak to me individually.

"Judy's parents contrasted that with their faith, and showed me Bible verses which reveal that God cares about each person individually, talks to them individually, and loves them unconditionally. They shared how they had complete assurance of their salvation the moment they accepted Christ as their personal Lord and Savior. I was especially impressed with the way Judy's father prayed. He sounded as though he were absolutely sure God was listening to his every word. He told me that he loved to pray and would pray for the whole two hours it took him to cut the grass. He would talk to God about his problems, about people he was concerned for, about all kinds of things. He said that since he started using his lawn-mowing time for prayer, he couldn't wait to get out the lawn-mower! I prayed, but I never enjoyed it like he did. I used to feel like I was praying to a deaf-mute.

"There were also some born-again people at my job, and they were talking to me at the same time. One of them gave me a book on how Mormonism doesn't teach what the Bible says. I read part of it, but it bothered me so I gave it back and said I had read it and that it didn't impress me. I didn't want to talk about it. Also, Judy's sister started seeing Judy every week after her Bible study, and she was also sharing Christ with her. I guess the Lord was trying to get at us in all kinds of ways! I remember wishing I could believe like Judy's father believed. But I didn't want to leave the security that I felt with my own family and my own church activities.

"Then, one night, as we were getting ready for bed, Judy started crying. She said she was lonely in the Mormon Church and didn't feel close to God anymore, like she had before we got married. She said she loved me and didn't regret getting married, but that she just knew there had to be more meaning to her faith in order for her to be happy. I found myself suggesting that we call her parents for advice. We woke them up, but they didn't mind. They shared with us about how to ask Jesus to make Himself real to us and to take charge of our lives. They didn't put down Mormonism (we already knew they didn't agree with it) but instead showed us how to find peace with God right where we were, mixed-up ideas and all."

REAL FREEDOM

"When Judy and I prayed to accept Christ that night I felt as though a giant weight had been lifted from my shoulders. Did I dare hope that God was accepting me? The next morning Judy and I prayed together to the Jesus we had accepted, and I knew that the Bible was true! I was a new man! I started reading my New Testament and got so excited about it that I made Judy come in and listen to me read it. We read all four Gospels in one morning. That evening we went to a Bible study with Judy's parents, and I felt as though I had finally come home. *This* was what had been missing. Jesus was wonderful!

"The next morning, a Sunday, we went to our Mormon service just like always. We really hadn't thought about leaving the Mormon Church at all. We thought our newfound faith would be compatible with our Mormonism. I especially didn't want to think about what my parents would do if we left the church. But halfway through the service we looked at each other and we both knew we had to leave. It was dead. God wasn't there. There was no life, no truth. Immediately after the service we left, went to my parent's house, and told them of our decision. My mother cried, my father yelled, and they both predicted that we would change our minds in a week. When we signed our resignations from the church two weeks later, my father told me he never wanted to see me or hear from me again. He was hurt and bitter.

"They refused to talk with us or see us for two years. Then, last year, when Judy had our little baby boy, my mother sent a card and a baby gift. We corresponded several times and also talked on the phone. Next week they're coming for a two-day visit. They've told us they won't talk about religion, that they're just coming to see their first grandchild. But we have so many people praying, and we're studying so hard, that we just know the Lord will give us an opportunity to share Jesus with them. When I first accepted Christ I thought it would be so hard to lose my family, and in fact that was what kept me from really listening to Judy's parents for so long. But now I'm confident that if my parents are willing to listen, they can have the same wonderful peace with God that we have. Jesus is worth all the family heartache."

Howard's parents didn't become Christians that weekend, but they did see that Howard and Judy were happy and growing spiritually. Howard reestablished a good relationship with his parents, and they correspond regularly now. His father has quit trying to criticize Howard's faith and has even defended him to Howard's brother at a family gathering where the brother was criticizing Howard's abandonment of Mormonism. Howard and Judy are convinced that God isn't through with Howard's parents yet.

5/ ANSWERS TO THE MOONIES

"Would you like to support our church youth group by donating something for this box of candy?" The short-haired young man stopped Jim Garrison as he was on his way down the hall to his office after lunch. At first he was startled. Who had given him permission to solicit inside the building? But then, the president of the company was a Christian. Maybe the kid was from the boss's church.

"I don't have much cash on me. Let me check. Here's five dollars. Hope it helps your youth group. What are you going to use the money for?"

"We help underprivileged kids in the cities. Thanks a lot. I have to go now." The young man's eyes glistened brightly under the artificial light in the building. Jim tucked the small box of peanut brittle under his arm and entered his office.

His secretary, Jack, greeted him with, "So you're a sucker too! You fell for the 'church youth group' line just like I did. Mr. Clark is going to kick that kid out of the building as soon as he can find him. Did you know he's a Moonie? Right in our own building, without permission, one of Sun Myung Moon's dupes. I don't know what turns people on to kooky religions.''

"Well, I guess I did fall for him. And I have heard some strange things about that Reverend Moon. I heard he brainwashes his converts and forces them to work 18 hours a day raising money for his own use. I think his followers believe he's like Jesus Christ. But I don't think all religious people are kooks. At least Mr. Clark is sensible enough to throw this guy out, and Mr. Clark claims to be a born-again Christian. Maybe I should find out more about the Moonies in case I run into one again. Don't want to get taken twice, you know!''

THE UNIFICATION CHURCH

There are many rumors about Reverend Sun Myung Moon and his Unification Church. There is an average of almost one article each week in the *Los Angeles Times* concerning some aspect of the Unification Church. Some rumors are true, some are not. While widespread recruitment of minors into Unification Church membership is not practiced, it is true that minors have joined the movement against their parents' wishes and they are very difficult to contact once within the organization. In August of 1980, a jury awarded $30,000 to the father of a girl who had joined the movement as a minor. The father's suit contended that the Unification Church violated his rights as a parent in recruiting her.[1]

Some ex-members charge that the indoctrination activities of the church make members unable to openly question what they are taught. Ex-member Gary Scharff, testifying in a San Francisco court case, said, "There is intense emotional pressure in which the individual is encouraged to repudiate his past life and even to repudiate the critical faculties developed in his previous life, to be more open to indoctrination."[2] It is important to know what the Unification Church stands for, and to have solid answers for the Moonie you meet.

UNIFICATION BEGINNINGS

Today's Unification Church claims a membership of over two million people. However, its history stretches back to the birth in North Korea in 1920 of Yong Myung Moon (later changed to Sun Myung Moon). He was born in the town of Kwangju Sangsa Ri, into a Presbyterian family. He went to high school in Seoul, South Korea, where he went to a Pentecostal church.

His calling to reveal God's will to the earth came on Easter morning, 1936, when Jesus Christ purportedly appeared to him and told him to "carry out my unfinished task." The magazine *A.D.* described how a voice then came out of heaven, saying, "You will be the completer of man's salvation by being the second coming of Christ."[3]

After study in Japan in electrical engineering, he returned to Korea and in 1946 founded the Broad Sea Church. He spent six months developing his theology (the "Divine Principle") and then returned to North Korea. He spent several years imprisoned by the Communists—some say because of his faith, but others because of immorality.

Moon returned to South Korea in 1950 with some of his followers and set up operations in Pusan. In 1954 he started the Holy Spirit Association for the Unification of World Christianity (one of the many aliases of the Unification

Church).* His capitalistic interests aided him in building a group of industrial businesses, which soon made him a millionaire.

The first Moon follower in the United States was a Korean, Miss Young Oon Kim, who came to recruit members in 1959. She was responsible for the first English translation of the *Divine Principle*. Today the American headquarters for the Unification Church is on a multimillion-dollar estate in upstate New York, near Barrytown. Other property is owned in New York, Oklahoma, Louisiana, California, Washington, and other states. Church recruitment is especially strong on college campuses, through the efforts of the Collegiate Association for the Research of Principles (CARP), a Unification Church front organization.

Although Moon and his followers claim that the Unification Church is compatible with and is in fact a development of Christianity, the two are in complete disagreement in almost all areas of teaching and practice. This is apparent to all who investigate the church's teachings. Even the secular magazine *Time* observed: "In essence, Moon's theology makes wide use of Biblical personae and events, but is no more than nominally Christian. Added ingredients are an odd mix: occultism, electrical engineering, Taoist dualism, pop sociology and opaque metaphysical jargon."[4]

Followers of Moon have been taught to "repudiate the critical faculties developed in his previous life to be more open

---

*Aliases include American Youth for a Just peace, C.D.C. Striders Track Club, Committee for Responsible Dialogue, Freedom Leadership Foundation, International Conference on Unified Science, International Cultural Foundation, International Federation for Victory Over Communism, International Re-Education Foundation, Korean Folk Ballet, One World Crusade, New Hope Singers International, Unified Family, and more.

to indoctrination." As Christians, we are commanded, "Do not treat prophecies with contempt. Test everything. Hold on to the good. Avoid every kind of evil" (1 Thessalonians 5:20-22). We must test the prophecies and revelations of Moon to see if they correspond to the Bible. If they do not, we must reject his message and give the answers of God's Word to the Moonies we meet.

UNIFICATION DOCTRINES

The Bible

"It may be displeasing to religious believers, especially to Christians, to learn that a new expression of truth must appear. They believe that the Bible, which they now have, is perfect and absolute in itself."[5]

The field of Biblical research is vast, and we cannot here adequately cover the many studies which reveal the trustworthiness of the Bible and its accuracy.[6] Neither do we have the space to discuss the inspiration of the Scriptures, based on the validity of Christ's resurrection.[7] However, if, as Moon claims, the Bible is compatible with Unification theology, then we can confidently turn to the Bible itself to see how it corresponds to what Moon says.

The Bible warns those who would add to God's Word: "Every word of God is flawless; he is a shield to those who take refuge in him. Do not add to his words, or he will rebuke you and prove you a liar" (Proverbs 30:5,6). That Moon contradicts the Bible proves that he is not God's spokesman and does not have new revelation. Whatever is revealed today must agree with what God has already revealed.

The perfect revelation of God and His requirements for man are in the Person of Jesus Christ: it is to Him and His words that we turn for ultimate truth, and not to Moon. Hebrews 1:1,2 declares the timeless relevance of God's revelation in Jesus Christ: "In the past God spoke to our forefathers through the prophets at many times and various ways, but in these last days he has spoken to us by his Son, whom he appointed heir of all things, and through whom he made the universe."

God

The Unification Church's authoritative publications say very little about the nature of God. However, Moon expressly denies the deity of Christ, and Moon's wife is referred to as the Holy Spirit! So we know that he rejects the Biblical doctrine of the Trinity. We will treat his error concerning Jesus Christ and the Holy Spirit separately below.

The Biblical doctrine of the Trinity is revealed in Scripture as the belief in only one true God (1 Corinthians 8:4-6) who exists eternally as three divine Persons (Luke 3:21,22): the Father (2 Corinthians 1:3), the Son (Romans 9:5), and the Holy Spirit (Hebrews 9:14; cf. Acts 5:3,4).

Jesus Christ

". . . this also does not signify that Jesus was God Himself. Jesus, on earth, was a man no different from us except for the fact that he was without original sin."[8]

"Jesus was born of a father and a mother, just as anyone else is, but in this case the Spirit of God was working also."[9]

There is a vast difference between Jesus Christ and all other men. Jesus Christ alone is the God-man, the second Person of the Holy Trinity, who was manifest in the flesh (John 1:14). Moon denies the two natures, human and divine, in Christ Jesus, even though this is the clear teaching of the Bible. Romans 1:3,4 distinguishes between the two natures of Christ, as does Romans 9:5, which declares, "Theirs are the patriarchs, and from them is traced the human ancestry of Christ, who is God over all, forever praised! Amen."

Philippians 2:1-11 gives the most clear picture of the two natures in Christ. It explains how Christ is to be our example of true humility. We are to humble ourselves before our brothers and sisters in Christ just as He humbled Himself to the Father and to all mankind. Verses 5-8 explain, "Your attitude should be the same as that of Christ Jesus: Who, being in very nature God, did not consider equality with God something to be grasped, but made himself nothing, taking the very nature of a servant, being made in human likeness. And being found in appearance as a man, he humbled himself and became obedient to death—even death on a cross!"

The divine Person who is the Word, the second Person of the Holy Trinity, eternal and uncreated, at a point in time took on an *additional* nature—that of a perfect man. He has always had a completely divine nature, and since His incarnation He has also had a completely human nature. The one divine Person has two natures, human and divine, and as God and man He serves as the perfect Mediator between God and man (1 Timothy 2:5).

Moon teaches that Jesus failed in His mission as the Messiah (see *Divine Principle* pp. 143-45). Jesus was supposed to accomplish man's spiritual and physical salvation by finding a perfect mate and founding God's perfect family on earth. However, according to Moon, the Jewish nation rejected Him and He was forced to "take the cross as the condition of indemnity to pay for the accomplishment of even the spiritual salvation of man."[10] This is why we need a "Lord of the Second Advent," like Sun Myung Moon. It is the duty of this Lord of the Second Advent to accomplish man's physical salvation. We will discuss this further when we discuss Unification salvation.

Jesus did not fail in his mission as the Messiah. It was God's predetermined will that Christ be sacrificed for our complete and full salvation. Acts 2:23,24 states, "This man was handed over to you by God's set purpose and foreknowledge; and you, with the help of wicked men, put him to death by nailing him to the cross. But God raised him from the dead, freeing him from the agony of death, because it was impossible for death to keep its hold on him."

Salvation is not a two-part process of first spiritual salvation and then physical salvation. Jesus accomplished it all, as we will see below in our discussion of Unification salvation.

Moon denies the virgin birth of Christ, but Matthew 1:18 declares, "This is how the birth of Jesus Christ came about. His mother Mary was pledged to be married to Joseph, but before they came together, she was found to be with child through the Holy Spirit." Verses 22 and 23 explain, "All this took place to fulfill what the Lord had said through the prophet: 'The virgin will be with child and will give birth to a son, and they will call him Immanuel'—which means, 'God with us.' " Verse 25 states clearly that Joseph had no union with Mary until she had given birth to Jesus.

The narrative of Luke 1:34,35 agrees with Matthew and contradicts Moon: " 'How will this be,' Mary asked the angel, 'since I am a virgin?' The angel answered, 'The Holy Spirit will come upon you, and the power of the Most High will overshadow you. So the holy one to be born will be called the Son of God.' "

The Unification Jesus Christ is not the Jesus Christ of the Bible. Moon's followers (Moonies) are carefully taught to mimic the vocabulary of the Bible. They sound just like Christians. They say they believe in Jesus Christ. They say they believe that Jesus Christ is their Savior. It is only when we know the facts about Unification theology that we discover that the Jesus Christ which the Moonies believe in is not the Jesus Christ of the Bible, and that the salvation offered by the Unification Jesus is only a partial salvation. When you give answers to the Moonie you meet, be sure that you require him to define his terms, to explain what he means. You too should carefully explain what you mean when you share God's Word with him.

The Holy Spirit

"There must be a True Mother with a True Father, in order to give rebirth to fallen children as children of goodness. She is the Holy Spirit."[11]

The Holy Spirit is not female or a mother, and the Holy Spirit is not the Father's "mate" for procreating children. A possible source for Moon's misconception regarding the Holy Spirit is the common Eastern presupposition of dualism—that God must be a pantheistic god, a union of opposites, a dualistic entity. God must encompass male and female, good and evil, etc. Moon's god has the True Father and the True Mother (the Holy Spirit), which are the male and female aspects of the typical Eastern dualistic and pantheistic god.

In distinction, the Bible describes God as distinctly separate from His creation (Romans 1:20-23), outside the realm of our existence (Isaiah 55:8,9; 66:1,2). The Bible describes God as apart from any generation or procreation in a sexual way. He is eternal (Revelation 21:6).

God the Holy Spirit is not human, much less female and Moon's wife. The Bible repeatedly describes God as spirit in distinction from human or animal. Job 37:23,24 states, "The Almighty is beyond our reach and exalted in power; in his justice and great righteousness, he does not oppress. Therefore, men revere him, for does he not have regard for all the wise in heart?" Isaiah 45:12 distinguishes between God and human by stating: "It is I who made the earth and created mankind upon it. My own hands stretched out the heavens; I marshaled their starry hosts."

Salvation

". . . his body was invaded by Satan, and he was killed. . . . In this manner, however devout a man of faith may be, he cannot fulfill physical salvation by redemption through Jesus' crucifixion alone."[12]

Unification salvation theology is completely opposed to the salvation theology of the Bible. Christ's death on the cross is complete, it can never be added to by anyone else, and it provides for the redemption of the whole person—body and spirit.

Romans 8:10,11 makes it clear that Christ accomplished our spiritual and physical salvation: "But if Christ is in you, your body is dead because of sin, yet your spirit is alive because of righteousness. And if the Spirit of him who raised Jesus from the dead is living in you, he who raised Jesus from the dead will also give life to your mortal bodies through his Spirit, who lives in you."

Romans 8 goes on to say that our immediate salvation from sin through the death of Christ on the cross guarantees us the ultimate "redemption of our bodies" (verse 23). We are not looking to be "adopted" by the True Father and True Mother (Messiah Moon and his Holy Spirit wife), and so inherit physical salvation in these same bodies. Instead we are looking forward to physical resurrection, to the time when we receive glorified, immortal bodies as a result of the work of Jesus Christ on the cross and through the power of

His own resurrection. First Corinthians 15:23 tells us that Christ's resurrection is the foretaste of our own resurrection. At His return (not Moon's debut), we too will be given resurrection bodies. First Corinthians 15:35-58 is not discussing the coming of some "Lord of the Second Advent," a Korean messiah like Moon. Instead, 1 Corinthians 15:35-58 proclaims the resurrection as being a result of "the victory through our Lord Jesus Christ" (verse 57).

Our salvation is complete in Jesus Christ. We do not need any second savior like Moon to finish the job. Christ's atonement on the cross is sufficient to save us fully. God deliberately ordained His appointment at the cross as the just action to accomplish our salvation. Romans 3:23-25 reads, "All have sinned and fall short of the glory of God, and are justified freely by his grace through the redemption that came by Christ Jesus. God presented him as a sacrifice of atonement, through faith in his blood."

The Bible makes no distinction between atonement for spiritual sin and atonement for physical sin. Jesus Christ has accomplished salvation both spiritually and physically. Hebrews 5:9 calls Jesus Christ "the source of eternal salvation for all who obey him." Hebrews 7:24,25 shows the full application of Christ's sacrifice: "Because Jesus lives forever, he has a permanent priesthood. Therefore he is able to save completely those whom come to God through him, because he always lives to intercede for them." Hebrews 10:10,12-14 states:

And by that will, we have been made holy through the sacrifice of the body of Jesus Christ once for all.

. . . But when this priest [Jesus] had offered for all time one sacrifice for sins, he sat down at the right hand of God. Since that time he waits for his enemies to be made his footstool, because by one sacrifice he has made perfect forever those who are being made holy.

We are not waiting for the revealing of Moon as our messiah, the "Lord of the Second Advent." There is no need for any sin to be cleansed anymore, for Jesus Christ did it all. The second advent that Christians anticipate is the second coming of Jesus Christ, not the coming of Sun Myung Moon. Christ's return will be publicly recognizable. (Revelation 1:7; 19:11-21) and will bring victory to believers and judgment to unbelievers (2 Thessalonians 1:7-10; Revelation 19:14-21).

Moon's brand of Christianity is a false brand. He may have been raised a Presbyterian, but his teachings place him outside the church of God. It is false Christs such as Moon against whom we are warned in 1 John 2:18,19:

> Dear children, this is the last hour; and as you have heard that the antichrist is coming, even now many antichrists have come. This is how we know it is the last hour. They went out from us, but they did not really belong to us. For if they had belonged to us, they would have remained with us; but their going showed that none of them belonged to us.

ANSWERS TO THE MOONIES

You can give these answers to the Moonie you meet. You can show him from God's Word that Sun Myung Moon is not his savior. You can give him the good news that Jesus already did everything necessary to give him a right relationship with God.

Many followers of Moon really desire to serve God. They are hungry for a personal relationship with a God who appears to be too far away. They often look to Moon as a father, one who can be a tangible representation of the God they don't know. You can share with them that God is as close as their prayer of repentance, that Jesus Christ is waiting to transform their lives and to give them eternal life. There is no intricate formula for performing works pleasing to God: Jesus said that the work pleasing to God is to "believe in the one he has sent" (John 6:29).

We can give the good news of salvation to the Moonie, echoing Paul's confident words in Romans 16:25,26:

Now to him who is able to establish you by my gospel and the proclamation of Jesus Christ, according to the revelation of the mystery hidden for long ages past, but now revealed and made known through the prophetic writings by the command of the eternal God, so that all nations might believe and obey him—to the only wise God be glory forever through Jesus Christ! Amen.

It is possible to reach followers of Moon with the gospel of Jesus Christ. In spite of all the sophisticated indoctrination and education programs of the Unification Church, there are Moonies who have left the church and found new life in Christ. Those who break away from Moon and search the Bible for themselves find that the God, the Jesus, and the salvation found in the Bible are infinitely more satisfying than those of the Unification Church.

DALE'S STORY

Dale was a young man who left the Unification Church after his parents convinced him to listen to a Christian minister talk about the differences between the Unification Church and Biblical Christianity. Dale had been a college freshman before he joined the Unification Church. He stayed in the church for two years before he decided that it was not the truth. During that time he had seen his parents only three times. He was afraid they would try to trick him out of it or even try to deprogram him.

On Dale's first trip home, his mother had spent the whole time crying and saying he was breaking her heart. His father had spent the whole time yelling at him and threatening to make him pay back his freshman tuition at college. On his second trip home, a year after he had become a follower of Moon, his parents were so glad to see him and so afraid that he would never come home again that they had refused to talk to him about anything religious at all. They had all been uncomfortable: Dale because he could sense his parents' fears under their calm facades, and his parents because they were afraid that at the first wrong move they would lose their son forever. The only positive result of that second trip was that Dale left feeling he could correspond with them without their threatening him or attempting to kidnap and deprogram him.

Over the weeks of correspondence after that second visit, Dale began to notice a difference in his mother's letters. She had begun attending a class on the cults at her church, and as her understanding of Dale's situation grew, her attitude toward him began to be more sympathetic. Her teacher had stressed the fact that people join cults in order to meet personal needs, and this one point was very significant to Dale's mother. Instead of continuing to feel that Dale was punishing his parents for their treatment of him, she saw that he had very real personal needs that he hoped could be solved by joining the Unification Church. He wasn't trying to get back at her, but was just trying to fulfill himself. Her letters began to reflect genuine concern for him and his problems.

Dale welcomed his mother's love and concern. He felt that, for the first time, she was taking an interest in him as a person. She was genuinely concerned about his goals, ideas, and fears. For once she wasn't trying to push him into fulfilling her own dreams but was interested in *his* dreams. Repeatedly his mother wrote that, although she didn't agree with his involvement with Reverend Moon, she loved Dale and respected him as a person with individual rights. She wrote that her love was unconditional and that he could always count on her, no matter what happened to him.

HOME AGAIN

Dale looked forward to his third trip home. He knew that things would be different this time. His mother was no longer fearful to the point of shutting him out. He was convinced of his parents' love for him and their acceptance of his goals, even though they disagreed with them.

And he was tired. He had been part of the small group of Unification Church members who raised money for the church by public solicitation. His dedication to the church meant everything to him and he pushed himself hour after hour, spending an average of 18 hours each day soliciting donations in exchange for the roses or artificial flowers or candy which the church gave him to use. His personal goal was to surpass the top member of his team, and, with a daily average take of over 400 dollars, he was well on his way to meeting his goal.

He had set this goal when he found himself thinking wistfully of his home, his old friends, and his family. When he caught himself wishing he could quit and go home, he knew he had to discipline himself. If God's truth really was in the Unification Church, he had to stay. He set his personal solicitation goal, told no one of his doubts, and redoubled his efforts to conform to the rest of the "family." He even told himself that he wasn't going home to rest, but was just going home to help his parents see the wonderful spiritual truths he had seen.

His first evening home was wonderful. His mother had made all his favorite foods for dinner, and he ate until he was stuffed. He hadn't realized that his diet had deteriorated so badly while he was on the road. He had been used to one meal each day, usually meatless, and usually a rice and vegetable mixture which one of the women had made. After dinner he and his father sat on the porch and talked about his father's farming. Gradually the talk ceased as both men enjoyed the quiet night. Dale realized that he hadn't relaxed like this in months—no, in the two years he had been in the Unification Church. He felt guilty, but the effects of the heavy meal and the quiet night kept him from moving. The next thing he knew, his father was waking him to go to bed. For the first time in two years he had no nightmares.

The next morning Dale's guilty feelings resurfaced. There was no time to waste, as he had last night. If necessary, he would cut his weekend visit short and return to the streets to show his dedication. It had been a mistake to think he could talk to his parents. But at breakfast his mother changed his mind. "Dale, you know that your father and I don't agree with your religious views and your involvement in the Unification Church. We don't like how you've changed over the last two years. But you also know that we love you and that we'll keep on loving you forever. I want to understand your commitment to Moon and I want you to understand why we're worried about you. Would you be willing to meet with my class teacher this afternoon to talk? We won't force you, and he's a nice, quiet man. But I think that we can do a lot for our relationship together if we can understand each other's perspectives. If you will agree to this afternoon's discussion, I promise that we won't ever discuss your involvement with Moon again unless you want to. Won't you just share that much with us?"

Dale didn't know how to answer her. Where was Dave, the church member who had helped him since the beginning? How should he answer his mother? What if the teacher was one of those deprogrammers? What if it was a trick? But then again, he had wanted to talk to his parents this weekend. That was how he had justified his trip home. He decided to trust his mother. "All right, Mom, I'll talk to him. But don't think it will change my mind. I know what I believe. I'm just doing this to make you happy, and I also want a chance to give my side of it."

TALKING AND THINKING

The afternoon discussion went long into the night. At first Dale refused to listen to anything the teacher had to say. He feigned attention politely, but as soon as the teacher paused, Dale would jump in with more words about how wonderful the Unification Church was, how terrible the world situation was, and how Reverend Moon has been chosen by God to bring spiritual light to a darkened world.

After a while, though, Dale started studying the teacher and his methods. He wasn't at all like a wildly ranting deprogrammer—the type of opposition he had been taught to expect. He calmly talked with Dale, systematically examining the teachings of the Unification Church and comparing them to the Bible. He didn't force Dale to agree with him, but he did ask Dale to explain when he didn't agree. This put Dale in an awkward spot. He knew, inside, that Moon was right. But somehow the responses he had learned by rote in the church weren't sufficient answers for the teacher. He wanted Dale to think through his own answers and to respond spontaneously. For the first time Dale had to think carefully about what he had accepted previously without question. As their discussion progressed, the precepts of Reverend Moon seemed less and less reasonable and appealing.

Then the teacher began contrasting Dale's life in the Unification Church to life in Christ. As Dale saw that in Jesus he could have immediate peace with God, close communion with God, clear-cut and noncontradictory guidance from the Bible, and immediate assurance of his salvation, he felt almost irresistibly drawn away from his allegiance to Moon and toward the Jesus of the Bible.

THE RIGHT DECISION

Dale received Christ as his Savior that evening and never went back to the Unification Church. The first few months of his Christian walk were difficult ones, and he sometimes longed to return to the security of Moon's fold, where he didn't have to think and didn't have to make his own decisions. But as the months went by he knew that freedom carried with it responsibility, and that freedom wasn't really worth very much without this responsibility. And no matter how difficult situations were, he knew that he could depend on the God of the universe to stand with him and give him all the help he needed.

6/ ANSWERS TO THE HARE KRISHNAS

Claudia hurried up to the department of motor vehicles building, rummaging through her purse for her registration renewal form. She hoped the line wouldn't be long, so she could still have some of her lunch hour left to grab something to eat before rushing back to class. She was a junior at a small Bible college in the Midwest.

"Lord," she thought, "why a line today when I'm in a hurry?" The line stretched from the counter, through the front door, and partway down the sidewalk. So much for lunch today!

Suddenly a young woman was in front of Claudia, holding out a sandwich of bean sprouts, avocado, and tomato. "Would you like a nice sandwich to eat while you wait? It's only $1.50 and the money goes to our educational endeavors. Can I get you some carob cookies, too?"

At first Claudia brightened—a solution to her lunch problem. But she was also cautious. She had been a victim before of donating to some cause she didn't like simply because she didn't ask about it. "Just what educational endeavors are these? Who do you represent?''

''We have a school where we study different cultures. It's a school for all ages, including classes for children. We represent ISKCON, and remember, the sandwiches are only $1.50. Which kind would you like?''

Claudia hesitated. Somewhere she had heard of ISKCON. What did the letters stand for? Ignoring the young woman's hand, stretched out toward her holding the sandwich, Claudia asked, ''What does ISKCON stand for? What does it mean? What do you call yourselves?''

The young woman's hand dropped. With reluctance mirrored in her face she replied quietly, ''It's the International Society for Krishna Consciousness. We're nonprofit, you know.''

''Oh, the Hare Krishnas! I knew I heard of you before. We studied about your group in our contemporary religions class. I'm sorry, but I'm a Christian and I don't care to support your religion. Thank you anyway.''

The girl persisted. She looked around, as if hopeful that the other potential customers in line weren't listening. ''But we believe in Jesus. We revere him very highly. He was the Son of God. As a Christian, don't you want to help support and feed the poor children who are orphaned and starving in India?''

CLAUDIA'S ANSWERS

Claudia silently thanked God for her class in contemporary religions and confidently replied, ''I don't doubt that you believe in the existence of Jesus, but as a devotee of Krishna, you believe that Jesus was only one person who had religious truth. You believe that he's a son of God, not the only Son of God. And you don't believe that He died for our sins. You believe in reincarnation and that you have to work out your own salvation from your bad karma by your devoted service to and worship of Krishna. I respect your right to hold your beliefs, but I don't agree with them and I don't appreciate your trying to make me think that Krishna and Christ are somehow compatible.

"As for the starving children in India, I would happily donate to help them. But I wouldn't donate to a religion whose beliefs supported and even produced that starvation because of belief in karma, that what each person experiences in this life is deserved as a result of his karma from previous lives.

"You know, you don't have to chant and work to please God. God loves you and knows that you could never do enough to reach Him on your own. That's why He sent His Son, Jesus Christ, to die for your sins. You're not bound to your bad karma—Jesus took it all on the cross and offers you forgiveness for all your sins for all time. You can have peace with God right now and know that He loves you and will take care of you. Could we sit down over there and talk some more?" Claudia had completely forgotten about her car registration. She enthusiastically grabbed the young woman's hand and started for a bench at the side of the building.

The Hare Krishna pulled away suddenly. She backed away from Claudia and clutched her sandwich close. "I don't want to talk. You can believe what you want to. Just leave me alone. I'm too busy to talk!" she blurted out as she quickly turned away to a man further down the line. The man shook his head at the offer of a sandwich and said, "I'm not religious, like that girl you were talking to, but I've heard about the Hare Krishnas and I don't want to have anything to do with you people. Just leave us alone. I don't know why the DMV lets you solicit here."

As the Hare Krishna moved down the line Claudia watched

and prayed silently for her. She hadn't been able to say much, but she prayed that the Lord would help the girl to remember what she had heard about God's love and Jesus' gift of eternal life to her. If only the lonely people would realize that it was easy to find peace with God!

THE HARE KRISHNAS

Members of the International Society for Krishna Consciousness (ISKCON), while comparatively few in number, are highly visible. This is because they are often robed in Indian dress and perform their religious chants in public places. Their solicitation practices are well known, and almost everyone has encountered them on a number of occasions in various public places. While no official statistics are available, estimates put the total American ISKCON membership at around 10,000. The organization is very wealthy; it maintains centers or ashrams throughout the United States and has several lavish temples in the West and the East.

The Hare Krishnas are a sect of Hinduism and embrace the basic doctrines of Hinduism. Although they claim to be compatible with Christianity, there is nothing at all Christian about their belief system.

In the polytheistic world of Hinduism, there are many sects that have chosen to worship one god or goddess more than the others. Vishnuism is that sect of Hinduism which worships Vishnu as the Supreme God. Krishnaism is a development of Vishnuism, teaching that Krishna is the supreme God who manifested Himself as Vishnu, rather than the traditional view that Vishnu manifested Himself as Krishna. Krishnaism was developed by Chaitanya Mahaprabhu, born in 1486, in the Bengal region of India. He practiced the *bhakti* form of yoga (path to God), which consisted of open and continual expressions of devotion to Lord Krishna. This, he believed, was the quickest way to *nirvana* (becoming one with the impersonal God) through erasing the debts of *karma* (the Hindu belief that all actions in one's life either credit or debit his account toward reaching nirvana; the debits must be worked off or credited with approved actions through multiple lives, or reincarnations).

The Hare Krishnas today still practice vocal and physical worship of Krishna as the sure path to nirvana. The vocal worship is the chanting of a mantra, or spiritual key, by which members recall and experience their knowledge of Krishna. The mantra for the Hare Krishnas is: Hare Krishna, Hare Krishna, Krishna Krishan, Hare Hare, Hare Rama, Hare Rama, Rama Rama, Hare Hare. Each follower is expected to chant at least 16 "rounds" a day. (Singing the mantra once on their 108 prayer beads equals one round.) Worship also takes place in the temples, where the multicolored statues of the deities are ceremoniously bathed, dressed, fed, and worshiped.

KRISHNA IN THE UNITED STATES

The Krishna movement came to the United States in 1965 in the teachings of Abhay Charan De Bhaktivendanta Swami Prabhupada (1896-1977), a well-educated Indian devotee of Krishna who followed in the footsteps of his own teacher, Bhaktisiddhanta Saraswati. Prabhupada founded the International Society for Krishna Consciousness and was its autonomous leader until his death, in 1978. After his death the Society was ruled by two different groups of men: a board of directors who run the administrative portion of the movement, and a group of 11 disciples who direct (sometimes at cross-purposes and in conflict with each other) the spiritual matters in the movement.

Today the Hare Krishnas have an extensive publishing operation, traveling "cultural" exhibits (which purport to present the culture of India but which are actually used for member recruitment), a massive fund-raising program, regular feasts and celebrations open to the public, and lavish temple and farm holdings. The best-known publications of ISKCON are the *Bhagavad-Gita, As It Is* and the periodical *Back to Godhead.*

The ISKCON solicitation practices have come under strong attack by the public. At their worst, such practices are described by critics as fraudulent con games. The Krishnas' philosophy is that money (called "laksmi," after one of Krishna's consorts) is being held captive by "karmis," or nonmembers, and that it is the duty of Krishna's devoted followers to "liberate laksmi." A karmi who gives money to ISKCON, whether willingly or unwillingly, knowingly or unknowingly, is burning off some of his karma and so is benefited spiritually. NBC News interviewed one Krishna girl.

Reporter: When seduction doesn't work, the Krishnas resort to con games. They even have a name for it—transcendental trickery. What does that mean?

Devotee: Well, we don't use that term but if it was called transcendental trickery, well, transcendental means God.

Reporter: And trickery means?

Devotee: That's self-explanatory.

Reporter: So it would be deception in the name of God.

Devotee: Not deception. Trickery isn't deception.

Reporter: What is it?

Devotee: It's trickery.

Reporter: Is that legitimate?

Devotee: If God's doing it, yes.

Reporter: And are you doing His work here?

Devotee: We're representing God.

The same news program interviewed an ex-member, Jenny Ayres, who explained the presupposition behind the Krishnas' practices:

Reporter: What our former Krishna Jenny Ayres explained to us is that Krishnas are taught that all non-Krishnas are demons and that they can do anything in dealing with demons because they have a higher morality. They're also taught that taking money from demons is a way of saving them, because they are putting that money to less sinful purposes. Now the Krishnas say they can't have control over each individual member in each individual airport, but we must say we went to airports across the country, to several airports, and found the same pattern at each airport.[1]

As Christians, we cannot condone such behavior. Second Corinthians 4:1,2 declares:

Therefore, since through God's mercy we have this ministry, we do not lose heart. Rather, we have renounced secret and shameful ways; we do not use deception, nor do we distort the word of God. On the contrary, by setting forth the truth plainly we commend ourselves to every man's consciences in the sight of God.

KRISHNA DOCTRINES

God

"In the beginning of the creation, there was only the Supreme Personality Narayana. There was no Brahma, no Siva, no fire, no moon, no stars in the sky, no sun. There was only Krishna, who creates all and enjoys all.

"All the lists of the incarnations of Godhead are either plenary expansions or parts of the plenary expansions of the Lord, but Lord Sri Krsna is the original Personality of Godhead Himself."[2]

ISKCON denies the Biblical doctrine of the Trinity, and, from a Hindu standpoint, denies a personal distinction between God and the creation. Hinduism's pantheism is a study in opposites. While maintaining that God is all and all is God (classic pantheism), Hinduism also believes in the existence of many gods. On top of that, Hinduism also teaches that the one supreme personality of the universe contains all of these gods and goddesses within him. Man's goal is to merge with that one supreme personality and relinquish his own personality. The Hindu concept of deity is both personal and impersonal.

Without discussing Hinduism in depth, we can easily see that Hinduism and Christianity are not compatible at all but are mutually exclusive. The Bible teaches that there is only one true God (Isaiah 43:10), who is distinct from His creation (Romans 1:20-23). Isaiah 44:6-20 condemns any idol worship, saying in part, "All who make idols are nothing, and the things they treasure are worthless. Those who would speak up for them are blind; they are ignorant, to their own shame."

The Bible also teaches that the one true God exists eternally as the three divine Persons of the Trinity: the

Father, the Son, and the Holy Spirit. A more thorough discussion of the Trinity appears in Chapter 3 of this book, "Answers to Jehovah's Witnesses," and we will discuss the deity of Christ below.

All the attributes of personality are resident in God. He is not a mere cosmic force or an impersonal spiritual entity. We will never become God or a part of God. The self-deification of ISKCON followers who attain nirvana is strictly opposed by the Bible. (Remember that it was Satan who promised deity to Eve in the Garden of Eden—Genesis 3:1-5). Ezekiel 28:2-9 reads in part, "Because you think you are wise, as wise as a god, I am going to bring foreigners against you, the most ruthless of nations; they will draw their swords against your beauty and wisdom and pierce your shining splendor. They will bring you down to the pit, and you will die a violent death in the heart of the seas. Will you then say, 'I am a god,' in the presence of those who kill you? You will be but a man, not a god, in the hands of those who slay you." Isaiah 47:8-11 also specifically denies the deification of man.

Jesus Christ

"Jesus is the Son, and Krsna is the Father, and Jesus is Krsna's Son."[3]

"Is not Jesus God? Brother, why do you want to kill God . . . you wish to 'kill' the One He loves by calling Him Jesus, the Father. But no one can end the love affair between Jesus and His Father, Krsna, by such perverted thinking."[4]

Again, the contradiction between the Bible and ISKCON is evident. The Bible teaches that Jesus Christ is uncreated and is eternally in a personal relationship with the Father and the Holy Spirit, all three divine Persons sharing the one divine nature.

Jesus Christ is God, as the Scriptures abundantly attest (John 1:1; 5:18; 8:58; 20:28; Titus 2:13; Romans 9:5; 1 John 5:20; Hebrews 1:8; etc.).

Philippians 2:1-11 reminds us that Jesus Christ, while eternally existing as God, humbled Himself and took on an additional nature, that of a man, and then humbled himself further by dying for our sins. He is not the product of one of Krsna's sultry affairs: He is eternal God in human flesh.

The Holy Spirit

". . . we must also develop a heart full of this love and follow the instructions of the Lord within our hearts—the Paramatma or 'Holy Ghost.' "[5]

The Holy Spirit of ISKCON is almost completely ignored, except when he is compared to a divine sort of intuition or God-consciousness within each man. This impersonal Holy Spirit is certainly not the third Person of the Biblical Trinity.

However, the Bible reveals to us that the Holy Spirit is a divine Person (Acts 5:3,4) who is distinct in Person from the Father and the Son (John 14:16,17) and is eternal (Hebrews 9:14).

While it is true that the Holy Spirit lives personally within each believer (Romans 8:9), He does not indwell us as an impersonal divine intuition. Instead, He is our Counselor, our Judge, our Guide, and our Teacher (John 16:5-15).

Mankind

"We understand the living entity, then, to be soul, consciousness, reincarnated in many bodies through many different births. The soul is of a superior nature to the body. Its nature is that of a superior nature of the body . . . . KRSNA, the Personality of Godhead, is the whole, the individual living beings are His parts and parcels . . . ."[6]

We will Biblically refute the doctrine of reincarnation in our treatment of ISKCON salvation (below), and deal here with the central ISKCON teaching concerning man.

ISKCON teaches that man is a part of Krsna, and that each man is individually part of God. As we discussed in our section dealing with the nature of God, man is not a part of God and can never be a part of God. There is an eternal distinction between the created and the Creator. If, as ISKCON teaches, man is a part of God, then man's goal should be to realize that intrinsic deity. However, we would then face a logical dilemma: how can anyone know if he has reached God-consciousness? At God-consciousness, the individual gives up the illusion of individuality and merges with the all-encompassing Person of Krishna. But he can never know if he has reached that point, because self-cognizance presupposes one's individual personality. Picture it this way: if I were striving for God-consciousness, I could never say, "I have reached God-consciousness." As soon as I say "I" I have disproved my claim, for I am still an individual personality. In fact, as soon as I even *think* "I" I have personalized myself in distinction from the rest of existence. To take it all the way back to the beginning, as soon as I *think* at all, I have performed an individual act of personality. Logically followed, the experience of Nirvana becomes a nonexperience experienced by a nonentity. This is impossible.

Salvation

"Sin is cleansed by personal sacrifice and discipline: 'All these performers who know the meaning of sacrifice become cleansed to sinful reactions.' "[7]

"To get rid of the ignorance one must practice

disciplinary devotion, by chanting the name of God, hearing and singing his praises, meditating upon the divine play and deeds of KRSNA, and engaging in the rites and ceremonies of worship. One must also repeat the name of God to the count of beads."[8]

Salvation in Krishnaism is thoroughly entwined with the Hindu concept of karma, or retributive justice. This teaching, which requires belief in reincarnation and/or transmigration, says that one's deeds, good and bad, are measured and judged either for or against him. Only when his good deeds have "atoned" for his bad deeds (and he is thus completely cleansed of this evil world) can he realize his oneness with Krishna and cease his cycles of rebirth.

The idea of karma and reincarnation is neither logical nor Biblical. Is it just or reasonable for a man to suffer in this life or be required to atone for sins in this life that he committed in a previous life that he doesn't even remember? How can suffering for an unknown sin reform the sinner and mature him to the point where he no longer performs that sin? Such so-called justice is cruel and absolutely opposed to the God of the Bible.

According to the Bible, salvation is not a result of our own works but rests solely on the cross work of Jesus Christ. We do not have to endure thousands of years of reincarnation to attain salvation; we can appropriate it immediately by trusting the Lord of our salvation, Jesus Christ. Hebrews 7:25 tells us that "he is able to save completely those who come to God through him, because he always lives to intercede for them." Ephesians 2:8-10 reminds us that salvation is by grace, not by any work on our part. John 6:29 declares that the work of God is to "believe in the one he has sent." We do not look forward to many lives of ignorant slavery to immutable karma; instead, we look forward to resurrection with Jesus Christ as our forerunner (1 Corinthians 15:23).

Christ rose from the dead to show us that we can have eternal life through His sacrifice. We don't have to grope blindly for God; Jesus showed us the way "so that men would seek him and perhaps reach out for him and find him, though he is not far from each one of us" (Acts 17:27).

This message of salvation in Jesus Christ is the core of our answer to the Hare Krishna. While Scriptural arguments can work as a part of our evangelism, the Krishna does not accept the fact that the Bible is God's infallible Word, and so he will not necessarily be convinced by our appeals to the Bible to disprove his doctrines. However, he is working as hard as he can to erase the debts of his karmic existence. He is earnestly striving to meet God's approval and to achieve salvation. We can offer him that salvation instantly. He can know for sure that he is a child of God and that all of his sins are forgiven him. They will not come back to haunt him. He will be forever free. "Jesus replied, 'I tell you the truth, everyone who sins is a slave to sin. Now a slave has no permanent place in the family, but a son belongs to it forever. So if the Son sets you free, you will be free indeed'" (John 8:34-36).

MARY'S STORY

Mary Oates had tried several different religious groups before she joined the Hare Krishnas in 1975. Although she had been raised a Roman Catholic, she became interested in Eastern thought and mysticism while still in high school. She had attended several Christian Science meetings as a sophomore, hoping to heal a skin disease that wasn't responding to treatment by her doctor. Christian Science told her that she could be healed if she would only appropriate the truth that disease and the whole material world didn't exist. She tried, and eventually the skin problem cleared up, but she wasn't at all convinced that it was because the material world didn't exist. Mary was drawn to the mystical elements of Christian Science, but wasn't comfortable with what she considered its conformity to middle-class America.

She thought she had found the ideal religion when she was a junior in high school. One of her physical education teachers was deeply involved in yoga and taught a yoga class at the community center on Saturday mornings. Mary first attended because she thought it might help her in gymnastics, but as she spent time talking with her teacher after class, she enthusiastically embraced the Eastern world view from which yoga sprang. At her teacher's invitation, she took a Transcendental Meditation (TM) course. Through some of the people at the TM center she was introduced to the Hindu scriptures, the Vedas, and it was in them that she first heard of Lord Krishna.

After Mary graduated from high school, she was in a sort of limbo. She didn't know if she wanted to go to college right away, as her parents wished, or if she really wanted to work full-time. She joined a community gymnastics team and spent most of the summer practicing with the team for the community fair to be given at the end of August. At the fair she found the Hare Krishnas. They performed an Indian religious ritual dance just after the gymnastics performance, and Mary was impressed with their sober dedication to the concepts she had been reading and enjoying in the Vedas. They told of their humanitarian activities after their dance and invited all who were interested to a feast the next day at their temple in Los Angeles.

ANSWER TO A QUEST?

Mary went. Here was what she had been looking for. She could serve others, learn in special classes, and show her devotion to God in tangible, elaborate religious rituals. She wasn't quite comfortable with the concept that she would eventually become part of God, but she readily embraced the active worship of God that was represented in Krishna. The temple members urged her to become more and more involved until, after just one month, she left her family and moved into the temple. She still visited them regularly, but each time she did, she was struck with the complete disparity between her old life and her new. At home, as the wealthy only child, she was often the center of attention and needed never lift a hand in any work. Her parents' primary concerns were with business and high finance. They didn't have time for religious devotion or philosophical discussions. When she mentioned this to her teacher at the temple, the older woman urged Mary to stop seeing her family. They weren't believers anyway. This was a hard decision for Mary to make, since her family had always been very close. But she never had to make the decision.

The day after her talk with her teacher, Mary was moved to Idaho to start a new temple. She didn't have time to tell her family where she was, and once she got to Idaho she was told that it was best to forget the past and the world, and to devote herself wholly to the worship and service of Krishna. She didn't have time to write them anyway. Her days were long—12 hours of canvassing the Boise public places for donations—and her nights were almost as long. The only thing that she was short on was sleep. After helping her teacher solicit at the airport, the large hotels, or the convention center, she and her teacher (along with the four other women at the temple) had several hours of work to do each night remodeling their house into a temple befitting Krishna. After a quick dinner at 10:00, they still had two hours of prayer and instruction before they went to sleep at midnight. Morning prayer watch began at 4:00 A.M.

The only variation in that routine was on Sunday, when the temple hosted a public feast as a combination public relations and recruitment function. Mary and the other women cooked and served while the men served as hosts and ate with the guests. Anything left over was for the women. It was on Sundays that Mary had her only doubt. How could she reconcile the austere, strictly regulated, and chaste life of the temple with the opulent and lavish weekly feasts, and the sacred stories of Krishna's excessive sexual and battle conquests? She was glad when Sunday was over and she didn't have to think about this disparity.

THE FADING DREAM

A year later, in the Eastern U.S., while helping to open a new temple for the third time, Mary began to be disillusioned. Her health was bad, she was continually tired, and she was emotionally unstable. Always a shy person, she found it very difficult to solicit donations at the airport each day, as she was assigned to do. The last three months had been especially miserable because she had lost her partner and had to work alone. Before, she could usually persuade her partner to do the actual solicitation while she lugged the heavy Krishna books, which were given in exchange for donations. But now each day was one long ordeal of summoning the courage to approach people and ask for donations.

She had thought of just sitting in the airport during her shift and then going back to the temple at night, pretending that she had worked, but she had to turn all the money over to the temple leaders, and she knew they wouldn't believe that she couldn't get any donations while other temple women were bringing in hundreds of dollars each day. After an hour of soliciting, she would go into the ladies' room and cry until she could once more summon the courage to go out for another hour. If she hadn't been so concerned about pleasing God, she wouldn't have lasted even those three months.

As Mary pleaded for donations, she found herself fantasizing. She would imagine her parents getting off one of the incoming planes, putting their arms around her, and taking her home. She fantasized about her old boyfriend, imagining seeing him invite her into the airport restaurant for a candlelight steak dinner, a welcome change from her strict vegetarianism.

THE LONG RIDE HOME

During one fantasy, Mary imagined herself calling her mother, crying, telling her she wanted to come home, and her mother telling her to pick up her ticket there at the airport and come home. Only as she hung up the phone did she realize that she had actually called her mother and that her mother had actually said she would pay Mary's way home. She told herself that she wouldn't give in, that she would maintain her allegiance to Krishna. She pushed for donations for three hours straight, proving to herself and to Krishna that she could do it.

Mary decided to take a break, and she looked around for a place to sit down. She was near the ticket counter. She should go over and tell them to cancel her ticket so her mother could get her charge account reimbursed. She walked up to the agent. She asked if he had a ticket for her, purchased in Los Angeles. He held it out. She couldn't tell him to cancel it. She took it. He urged her to hurry because the flight was leaving in 20 minutes and the gate was on the other side of the airport.

She tried to calm her rapid heartbeat. She had to get control of herself. But, clutching her ticket to her tightly, she dropped her books and her money pouch and ran down the concourse. She didn't stop until she was on the plane with her seatbelt fastened. She didn't allow herself to think until the plane was in the air.

Then Mary panicked. What had she done? What would the elders say to her? How could they forgive her for leaving her books and money? What would they do to her for leaving without their permission? Wildly she looked around at the other passengers. She was sure that the temple elders already knew what she had done. They must have disguised themselves and followed her onto the plane. They would catch her and take her back. They would never let her be alone again. She had failed! She had failed in her devotion to Krishna, and it was all for nothing. She would never see her parents again.

BACK TO FREEDOM

She couldn't believe it when she saw her mother and father waiting at the gate as she got off the plane. Why had the temple allowed them to come? Why weren't they taking her away from her family? Why hadn't they grabbed her on the plane? It was only when she was in her own room at home, with her mother's arms around her, that Mary thought realistically. It was over. She was free! The months of exhaustion and emotional trauma were over. She began to cry and then sobbed on her mother's shoulder. She fell asleep, exhausted, two hours later, her mother's arms were still around her. She was home.

It is now three years since Mary was a member of ISKCON. She has become a Christian and now teaches Sunday school to five-year-olds at her community church. She has just finished her first year of college, majoring in social work. She still wants to help people, and she still wants to serve God. She hopes to be a missionary in India someday. As Mary says, "The God of the Bible is so much better and so much more real than Krishna. I don't have to fear my God. I just love Him and thank Him for the salvation He has given me in Christ."

7/ ANSWERS TO THE WAY INTERNATIONAL

"Pastor, we've just moved here and we wanted to talk to you because we had some problems before we came here, and we want some help." The young man leaned forward in his chair in the pastor's study. His hands gripped those of his wife, a shy blonde with a hesitant smile.

Pastor Bob Grant leaned forward, toward Jacki and Jerry Glen. "You know, Jerry, that I'll do whatever I can to help you both. It would help me if you tell me, in your own words, what you think your problem is."

"We're scared. Before we moved to Tucson we lived in Ohio. We were part of an evangelism team. We gave up two years to work evangelizing the world. We were called WOW ambassadors—that's the Word Over the World. It's part of a church group called The Way. I don't know if you've ever heard of it, but we joined it thinking that it was just some evangelistic part of the charismatic movement. We wanted more life in our Christian walk, and we thought that maybe getting into the charismatic movement would help. But The Way is different from what we were expecting. Our leader,

Victor Paul Wierwille, says that God gave him a special message for the church and the world. He says that true Christianity was lost early in church history and that God has given him the job of restoring the gospel message today.

"At first, we couldn't believe the love and concern all the members showed us. They fed us, housed us, shared the Bible with us, and helped us to learn to speak in tongues. When they gave us the chance to join their evangelism effort, we couldn't resist. They really lived what we considered a New Testament church life."

TRAPPED IN FEAR

"Before we knew it, we were in so deep that we couldn't see our way out. We had sold everything we owned and had given it to the church. After all, on a two-year missionary venture we wouldn't need anything. Then we lost touch with our families, partly because we were so busy, partly because we moved around so much evangelizing, and partly because they didn't understand our desire to serve the Lord and so started arguing with us."

Jacki took over with, "And then we began realizing that we weren't really preaching the gospel at all, but were just trying to sell people on The Way's publications and Wierwille's *Power For Abundant Living* courses. Every time we tried to question anything, we were told that we were going against God and not trusting the Lord in all things. When we took some advanced courses we found out that Wierwille doesn't believe that Jesus is God. He also believes that judgment will come on the earth and that The Way will be persecuted. We heard rumors that The Way was preparing to arm itself against attack.

"Toward the end we lived in constant fear that we were into a cult, but at the same time we were afraid that it was

God's organization and that if we left, God would forsake us. Finally, in the middle of the night, Jerry and I took a walk after a meeting and just kept walking. We never went back. But we're still afraid. What if it is God's organization? What if God has condemned us? You don't know how much I want Jesus' love, but I feel like I've betrayed Him.''

Jerry interrupted, "We were so depressed, so scared, so bound while we were in The Way. Maybe it is God's organization today, but we can't take it anymore. I would rather be hiding in Tucson, fearful of God's wrath, than in The Way without a mind of my own."

THE REAL GUIDE

"Jerry and Jacki, do you really think that God, who is love, is behind all that fear and negativism that you found in The Way? Do you think that God would have given you minds with which to think and question and then given you a spokesman who would tell you never to question?" Pastor Grant held up his Bible, saying, "This is the only guide you need to find out God's will. You can depend on His Word in the Bible all the time. It will never let you down. It won't strike fear into your heart. It will bless you and show you clearly how to receive and live in God's ever-abundant love. Let's open the Scriptures together and see what God's will is for our lives."

Jerry and Jacki are not alone in their fear of The Way International. Many people who have left The Way went through months of self-doubt and fear.[1] Others leave the movement and drift aimlessly, rejecting The Way's claims but not willing to listen to the claims of true Christianity. Others leave the movement helped by concerned Christians who show them that an immediate and complete commitment to the Lordship of Jesus Christ can meet their needs while at the same time freeing them from bondage to the false teachings of The Way. Jerry and Jacki found the help they needed from a concerned Christian pastor who was able to show them, from the Bible, that the love of God is the answer to the fear they felt because of The Way (2 Timothy 1:7).

THE WAY INTERNATIONAL

The Way International was founded by Victor Paul Wierwille in the early 1950s. The exact date is hard to pinpoint, but we know from its founder's own writings that the germ of Way theology was developing as early as 1942, when he claimed that God the Father spoke to him and told him that if he would teach others, God would tell him the first accurate knowledge of the Bible since the first century.[2] His healing ministry began just a few years after that, and he was led "into the manifestation of speaking in tongues . . . and from that day in 1950 my life and ministry began to change very rapidly."[3]

During the fifties Wierwille began to be openly opposed to other churches, and resigned (some say under pressure) from the pastorate in the Evangelical and Reformed denomination. However, The Way International was a relatively small and insignificant cult until the early 1970s, when Wierwille and his small group of followers began to actively evangelize from among the Jesus movement. This practice of taking new membership from those already converted to Christ, a sort of "raiding the sheepfold," is still practiced today. This is one reason that most of The Way members, while having accepted false doctrines, are still Christians. The Way, through its recruitment methods, is one of the few cults with a largely Christian membership.

Second Corinthians 11:3,4 aptly describes the situation: "But I am afraid that just as Eve was deceived by the serpent's cunning, your minds may somehow be led astray from your sincere and pure devotion to Christ. For if someone comes to you and preaches a Jesus other than the Jesus we preached, or if you receive a different Spirit from the one you received, or a different gospel from the one you accepted, you put up with it easily enough.'' Your encounters with members from The Way can easily occur right in your own church or Bible study.

Victor Paul Wierwille, founder of The Way and a self-proclaimed dispenser of God's truth, was born in 1916 in New Knoxville, Ohio, where his organization is now headquartered. Although he claims an extensive educational background, no researcher has been able to substantiate his claim that he "took everything I could take at the Moody Bible Institute, too, through their correspondence courses."[4] Moody has no record of his completing any course through them. His doctorate was obtained at a "diploma mill" for a fee, with no formal instruction.

The Way Biblical Research Center is located on 150 acres near New Knoxville. The Way owns other property throughout the United States (almost all Way membership is American) and operates two schools for training its followers in Wierwille's doctrines. Current membership is approaching 100,000 active members, members who began their association with The Way through taking the self-help course *Power for Abundant Living*. This is one's introduction to the cult and is where prospective members are initiated into speaking in tongues.

The Way is tightly structured, its organization labeled around the symbol of a tree. Wierwille and his close advisors are called the roots of The Way tree; the trunk is an association of national bodies; state groups are called branches; limbs represent city groups; and the home studies are called twigs. Individual members are "leaves."[5]

THE WAY AMBASSADORS

Way "ambassadors," those members who recruit new members, do not say that they belong to a church or religious group (although The Way has dozens of ordained ministers) but to an organization dedicated to promoting the truth of God's Word:

> Its followers are people of every culture and ethnic background who all their lives have hungered for purpose, for meaning, for answers to life's enigmas, and for the power that would lead them into the fulness of Christ's promise: "I am come that ye might have life, and that ye might have it more abundantly." (John 10:10).[6]

The effect of this is to attract people who are dissatisfied with their spiritual lives, who want more from their church or their Christian walk. As Jerry and Jacki said, they just wanted to share Christ and they thought The Way would help them do that.

Every Way member is a "missionary" in the sense that he is always seeking to bring new members to the "truth" in The Way. There are also temporary full-time missionaries in The Way who give one year of their lives setting up new *Power for Abundant Living* courses throughout the world. They support themselves for that one year with only part-time work, and they call themselves WOW Ambassadors (The Word Over the World, The Way's ultimate goal).

The annual convention of The Way is called the Rock of Ages and is held at the Ohio headquarters. Thousands of members attend each year. It will probably be at this convention in 1982 that Wierwille's official successor will be named and installed over the cult. Wierwille has announced that his retirement will be in 1982, and observers within and without the group predict that his son, Don, will take the reins from his father. Trusted aid Craig Martindale is expected to continue the daily administration of the vast organization.

Wierwille publishes numerous books, among them *Jesus Christ Is Not God; Power for Abundant Living; Receiving the Holy Spirit Today;* and *God's Magnified Word.*

THE COUNTERFEIT WAY

Two characteristics stand out about The Way when it is compared to the Christian church: it is a clever and close counterfeit of the church, claiming to believe the Bible while denying its cardinal teachings; and it claims to manifest the *charismata,* or supernatural spiritual gifts, as described in 1 Corinthians 12 and other Bible passages.

It is not our purpose here to discuss whether the supernatural "sign" gifts of the early church are available to the church today. This is an important area of theology, but it is secondary in the sense that one's salvation is not dependent on his beliefs concerning the continuance of all the sign gifts in the church.

However, whether we as Christians accept their continuance or not, we can all agree that a cult such as The Way, which denies every essential doctrine of Scripture and which is led by a man who demands absolute obedience to his commands and claims to be the sole source of God's truth today, is not in a position to receive supernatural gifts from God. If the charismata are available for the church today, they must be manifested in and given to a body of believers actively committed to the cardinal teachings of the Bible. Whether or not there are any valid manifestations of the charismata today, we know that the manifestations in The Way are not from God but are counterfeit.

We also said that the group is a clever and close

counterfeit of the church, claiming to believe the Bible while denying its cardinal teachings. This is the way that false teachers can snatch away unwary members of the body of Christ. Paul warned of this, and we should take his warning to heart: "Even from your own number men will arise and distort the truth in order to draw away disciples after them. So be on your guard! Remember that for three years I never stopped warning each of you night and day with tears" (Acts 20:30,31). We will examine the beliefs of The Way and Victor Wierwille, and we will expose them as heretical teachings which place the organization outside the true church of God.

THE WAY DOCTRINES

The Bible

". . . Aramaic was the original language in which the New Testament was written. . . ."[7]

". . . The records in the Gospels are addressed at times to Israel and at other times to the Gentiles, but never to the Church of God. One of the greatest errors in the translation of the Bible was placing the four Gospels in the New Testament. The Gospels logically belong in the Old Testament."[8]

In addition, Wierwille claims that he properly interprets the Bible and preserves the meaning of the text, confident that it is God's infallible Word, but in practice he manipulates texts, adds words to them in brackets, and, if all else fails, claims that the original meaning was "lost" by the apostate church and that God has given it specially to him to reveal to the world. Such practices effectively makes the Bible little more than a tool in Wierwille's work to build his own system.

The New Testament was not originally written in Aramatic.

It was written in Greek, as careful study of the style and language pattern of the text clearly shows. Even if it had been written in Aramaic, it could not have been the Aramaic that Wierwille uses, which is from eastern Syria and did not even develop until the beginning of the third century A.D. As *The New Cults* points out, "Eastern Syriac Aramaic has some significant differences between it and early Palestinian Aramaic which makes it impossible to base philological arguments based on similarities."[9]

Wierwille gives the impression that what is "Old Testament" is extraneous to God's Word for the church, and can safely be ignored. Evidently, by placing the Gospels in the Old Testament he feels that one can thereby ignore those Gospel teachings which disagree with Wierwille's system. However, Jesus reminds us that even the Old Testament Scriptures testified of Him (Luke 24:25-27). He also said, "Do not think that I have come to abolish the Law or the Prophets; I have not come to abolish them but to fulfill them. I tell you the truth, until heaven and earth disappear, not the smallest letter, not the least stroke of a pen, will by any means disappear from the Law until everything is accomplished" (Matthew 5:17,18). The establishment of the church did not coincide with the disappearance of heaven and earth!

The Trinity

"That defines the doctrine of the trinity, and this I do not believe the Bible teaches. With all my heart I believe the Bible teaches that (1) God is the Father of our Lord Jesus Christ, that (2) Jesus Christ is the Son of God and that (3) God is Holy and God is Spirit . . . . In other words, I am saying that Jesus Christ is not God, but the Son of God. They are not 'co-eternal, without beginning or end, and co-equal.' ''[10]

Wierwille openly denies the Christian and Biblical doctrine of the Trinity. He teaches that only the Father is God; that the Son (Jesus) is a created being; and that the Holy Spirit is just another name for the Father (while holy spirit, lowercase spelling, is the spiritual nature given each man at his conversion).

Wierwille manipulates Scripture, appeals to obscure and faulty interpretations, mistranslates passages, and, if all else fails, claims that "the original was corrupted" in order to avoid the clear Biblical teaching about the Trinity. Although he has some novel methods of interpretation, his basic arguments against the Trinity are like those of the Watchtower (Jehovah's Witnesses).

As we explained in Chapter 3, "Answers to Jehovah's Witnesses," the Christian doctrine of the Trinity does not correspond to any pagan trinity ideas, even though that is Wierwille's claim. Outside of Christianity there is no belief in the Trinity as Biblically defined. Pagan trinities are usually *triads*—three gods supreme over all the rest. There are also pagan trinities that promote belief in a "family of God," consisting of a Father God, a Mother God, and a Son God. Still other pagan trinities fall into the error of modalism, seeing one God as possessing three main attributes, aspects, forms, or functions, each known by a different name. Modalism sees only one Person in the Godhead.

However, in Christianity we believe the Bible's own statements about the nature of God. The Bible teaches that while there is only one true God (or one God by nature) (Isaiah 43:10), this one God is eternally existent in three distinct Persons (Luke 3:21,22): the Father (Colossians 1:2), the Son (John 20:28), and the Holy Spirit (Hebrews 9:14; Acts 5:3,4). We do not believe in three Gods and one God, or in three Persons and one Person, or in some sort of schizophrenic God. The Father is neither the Son nor the Holy Spirit in Person; the Son is neither the Father nor the Holy Spirit in Person; and the Holy Spirit is neither the Father nor the Son in Person. Each is fully God, and yet the three eternally distinct Persons compose the one true God. Rather than being illogical, such a doctrine merely transcends the realm of our complete comprehension. However, the Scriptures teach it strongly, and we as Christians must believe it. We will discuss this further as we discuss Wierwille's beliefs concerning the Person and nature of Christ and the Holy Spirit.

Jesus Christ

". . . The Gospel of John established the truth of God's Word that Jesus Christ was the Son of God, not 'God the Son' or 'God Himself.' "[11]

"The Bible teaches that there is only one true God, that God was in Christ, that God is Spirit, and that God is eternal in contrast to Jesus, whose beginning was his birth."[12]

Wierwille's statements about the Gospel of John and the Bible in general are absolutely false. The Bible is abundantly clear that Jesus Christ is truly God, one with the Father in essence or nature. He is eternal, not created. John, perhaps more than any other book in the New Testament, repeatedly affirms Christ's deity.

John 1:1 opens with a declaration of Christ's deity: "In the beginning was the Word, and the Word was with God, and the Word was God." Wierwille tries to sidestep the clear meaning of this verse by providing his own "expansion" of the verse, adding 12 new words of his own to the verse: "In the beginning was the Word (God), and the (revealed) Word was with (*pros*) God (with Him in His foreknowledge, yet independent of Him), and the Word was God." Wierwille tries to make "the Word" in clauses one and three a different thing from "the Word" in clause two, to which he arbitrarily adds the explanation that this other "Word" wasn't really "there," but was just a part of God's thinking. Totally ignoring all Greek and textual scholarship, Wierwille struggles to take away the clear meaning of this verse. In addition, he completely ignores the rest of the passage, which repeatedly asserts the deity of the one Word under consideration, the Word identified in verse 14 as the Son of God.

John 1:1-14 repeatedly affirms the deity of Christ. In verse 1 He is said to already be existing "in the beginning." Renowned Greek grammarian A. T. Robertson comments on the verb "was" (*en* in the Greek): "Three times in this sentence John uses this imperfect of *eimi*, to be, which conveys no idea of origin for God or for the Logos—simply continuous existence. Quite a different verb (*egeneto*, became) appears in verse 14 for the beginning of the Incarnation of the logos."[13]

John 1:3 tells us that "without him nothing was made that has been made." There are only two classes of beings: those created and those uncreated. This verse says that the Word, Jesus, made all the created things. This requires that Christ Himself be uncreated. The Bible tells us that only the one true God is uncreated (1 Timothy 1:17).

John 1:4-9 calls the life-giving *Word* "light," shining in the darkness. The parallel passage in 1 John 1:1-7 calls *God* light.

John 1:10 reiterates that the Word was the Creator of the world. There is nothing in the context of the passage or of the Bible as a whole that would justify trying to identify two different beings as the Word in John 1.

John 1:11 states, "He came to that which was his own," and Psalm 78:52-54 declares that the Jews, of whom Christ was born, were *God's own* people. The verse read: "But he brought his people out like a flock; he led them like sheep through the desert. He guided them safely, so they were unafraid; but the sea engulfed their enemies. Thus he brought them to the border of his holy land, to the hill country his right hand had taken." This same theme, of God caring for His people like a shepherd for his sheep, is carried out in describing Jesus in John 10:1-20,25-30, culminating in another proclamation of Christ's diety in verse 30: "I and the Father are one." At this supposed blasphemy "the Jews picked up stones to stone him" (v. 31). First Corinthians 10:1-4 identifies the Leader of the Jews through the water in Egypt and in the desert as *Christ;* Psalm 78 identifies this same leader as *God.*

John 1:14 declares that the Word possessed a glory, "the glory of the one and only Son, who came from the Father, full of grace and truth." In Isaiah 42:8 God declares, "I am the Lord; that is my name! I will not give my glory to another or my praise to idols." Jesus must be God!

John 1:15 records John the Baptist as saying, "He who comes after me has surpassed me because he was before me." If the Word (according to Wierwille) only existed in God's foreknowledge before Christ's birth, and John was born at least six months *before* Jesus (Luke 1:25,26), then how could John say that Jesus existed before him?

We could go on through the rest of the Gospel of John, and even through the rest of the New Testament, showing the consistent testimony of Scripture that Jesus is God. Wierwille has mistranslated, misinterpreted, and manufactured verses to support his position. We have seen from a brief look at the context of John chapter 1 that the clear teaching of the Bible is that Jesus is Jehovah-God. We do not have to go further to prove that. (However, other verses dealing with the deity of Christ are discussed in the chapter on Jehovah's Witnesses).

The Holy Spirit

"The gift from The Holy Spirit, the Giver, is *pneuma hagion,* holy spirit, power from on high, spiritual abilities, enablements. This power is spirit in contrast to the senses. Spirit is holy as opposed to the flesh, which is called by God unholy. God is Holy Spirit and God can only give that which He is; therefore, the gift from the Giver is of necessity holy and spirit."[14]

Wierwille mimics two ancient heresies in his doctrine of the Holy Spirit. His teaching is modalistic in the sense that he identifies the Holy Spirit with the Person of the Father, who alone is God. Modalism confuses the Persons of the Trinity, seeing God as only one Person who may have different names or "modes." Wierwille is unitarian (somewhat like the Jehovah's Witnesses). He identified "holy spirit" (lowercase) with the impersonal spiritual gift of God the Father. Neither view is correct. Both are heretical and unscriptural.

The Bible teaches that the Holy Spirit is a Person, not an impersonal gift, and that His Person is distinct from that of the Father and the Son. He is the third Person of the Trinity and is fully God.

John 14:26 shows the personal distinctions among the Father, the Son, and the Holy Spirit. "But the Counselor, the Holy Spirit, whom the Father will send in my name, will teach you all things and will remind you of everything I have said to you." It is easy to see that the Holy Spirit is personally distinct from the Father and is fully a divine Person (one who teaches and reminds). This distinction is repeated in 1 Corinthians 2:10-12:

The Spirit searches all things, even the deep things of God. For who among men knows the thoughts of a man except the man's spirit within him? In the same way no one knows the thoughts of God except the Spirit of God. We have not received the spirit of the world but the Spirit who is from God, that we may understand what God has freely given us.

The numerous New Testament citations of Old Testament verses where the New identifies the subject as the Holy Spirit and the Old identifies the subject as God serve to show that the Holy Spirit is God. In Acts 5:3,4 Peter in one verse refers to the Holy Spirit and in the next verse identifies the Holy Spirit as God. The Holy Spirit is personal, is God, and is distinct personally from the Father and the Son. (Further information on the Holy Spirit is found in the chapter on Jehovah's Witnesses.)

Mankind

Concerning the fall of mankind—"The spirit is disappeared. The reason the spirit was called dead is that it was no longer there. Their entire spiritual connection with God was lost. From that very day Adam and Eve were just body with soul—as any other animal."[15]

Concerning man and physical death—"No passage of Scripture teaches that there is conscious existence after death. To teach and believe that man does not really die, but only "crosses the bar," entering a higher plane of life in existence with God, is propagating Satan's original lie in Genesis when he said, 'Ye shall not surely die.' The teaching that when a person dies he immediately goes to God in heaven is one of the many doctrines of Satan and his fallen angels."[16]

Wierwille says that no man until the day of Pentecost had

a spirit. Until that time man was just like the animals and could not have a personal relationship with God. At Pentecost, God gave the gift of "holy spirit" to the believers. This was not the Biblical gift of the Holy Spirit, through the agency of the Father and Son (Jesus spoke of this in John 14), but was the gift from the Father, who is holy and spirit and is therefore called the Holy Spirit, and consisted of the spiritual life that man had lost at the fall.

The Bible declares that man was always able to respond to the revelation that God gave him. He has always possessed a God-consciousness (in distinction from the animals) that made possible a relationship with God. Psalm 32:2 says, "Blessed is the man whose sin the Lord does not count against him and in whose *spirit* is no deceit." Ecclesiastes 12:7 clearly distinguishes between man and the animals by saying, concerning man's death, "and the dust returns to the ground it came from, and the spirit returns to God who gave it." Mary, the mother of Jesus, had a spirit that responded to God: ". . . my spirit rejoices in God my Savior" (Luke 1:47). Luke 1:15 speaks of John the Baptist as "filled with the Holy Spirit even from birth."

Wierwille has borrowed the doctrine of soul sleep (the idea that man is unconscious after death) from several cults (as Jehovah's Witnesses) who teach the same thing. He did not get it from the Bible. We have already mentioned Ecclesiastes 12:7. Wierwille ignores this verse and lifts Ecclesiastes 9:5 out of context to support his position. Ecclesiastes 9:5 speaks of the *appearance* of a man's body after death, when it *appears* to be asleep. It is not referring to man's spirit. This is paralleled in Ecclesiastes 3:20, whereas 3:21 indicates the distinction between the unconscious body and the conscious spirit.

New Testament verses which discuss the conscious existence of man after death include 2 Corinthians 5:6-8 and

Philippians 1:23. These verses are discussed in more detail in the chapter on Jehovah's Witnesses.

Salvation

". . . the only visible and audible proof that a man has been born again and filled with the gift from the Holy Spirit is *always* that he speaks in a tongue or tongues."[17]

". . . . Do we sin in the spirit? No. But in body and soul we fall."[18]

Wierwille teaches that salvation is by grace and apart from works. If that were as far as he went, we could agree with him. However, that salvation formula is but a prelude to his teachings concerning tongues and concerning sins.

Tongues are not the seal of our salvation. Without getting into a discussion of whether tongues are a valid manifestation in today's church, we will say that for anyone to manifest the Biblical gift of tongues, he must do it in accord with new Testament teaching on the use of the gift. Tongues have more than one function in the New Testament (1 Corinthians 12-14; Acts 10; etc.), but nowhere does the Bible say that tongues are a mark of one's salvation. In fact, tongues are a gift given by God to those who are believers already (1 Corinthians 12:27,28) for the edification of the believer and the church, and not as some sort of badge of salvation.

Wierwille's understanding of the Bible's teaching regarding sin is simplistic. While he claims that a believer cannot sin "in his spirit," he claims that he sins in body and soul. However, the Bible makes no such distinction. The Bible declares that the *person* sins, using his body to perform the sin. The body is not sinful in itself. It bears the marks of sin (Romans 8:21) and can be used by the person to perform sin (Roman 6:13), but those references to the body as sinning are simply literary forms of symbolism. To sin is to willfully disobey; something that is not personal has no will and therefore cannot choose to sin.

The result of Wierwille's teaching on sins is that his followers are able to perform all kinds of acts condemned as sinful in the Bible while claiming that they didn't sin in their spirits, but only in their bodies and their souls. There is little practical difference between what Wierwille teaches and the idea that a Christian can do anything with impunity. In fact, an ex-follower of The Way was quoted in *Eternity* magazine as saying, "They tell you that you can have free sex or do your own thing because you are born again and going to heaven. So, you can commit adultery."[19]

There are many passages in the Bible that contradict Wierwille's teachings concerning salvation and sinning. Romans 6:1,2,11-14 seems to be speaking against exactly the same ideas promoted by The Way:

What shall we say, then? Shall we go on sinning so that grace may increase? By no means! We died to sin; how can we live in it any longer. . .?

In the same way, count yourselves dead to sin but alive to God in Christ Jesus. Therefore do not let sin reign in your mortal body so that you obey its evil desires. Do not offer the parts of your body to sin, as instruments of wickedness, but rather offer yourselves to God, as those who have been brought from death to life; and offer the parts of your body to him as instruments of righteousness. For sin shall not be your master, because you are not under law, but under grace.

ANSWERS TO THE WAY

Having surveyed the teachings and practices of The Way, we can see clearly that The Way is not the way of the Bible.

The Way is a cult, with all the teachings and practices common to a cult. The main difference between The Way and most other cults is that The Way proselytes members from the real body of Christ. Christians are being deceived by its false teachings. We need to be ready to give God's answers to our fellow Christians who are caught in this deception.

How can you answer The Way when you meet a member, perhaps in your own church or Bible study? The pattern for action is the same as for other cultists: with prayer, love, accurate information, sound Bible knowledge, and a willingness to help the cultist find that his needs are met in Jesus Christ, rather than in Wierwille's man-made organization.

Be on guard for the faulty Bible interpretations which The Way follower has been taught. We have examined Wierwille's teachings on essential doctrine, but he is also in error on even such details as how many men were crucified with Christ. Everything a Way follower has been taught should be suspect. Keep turning to the Word of God and studying it in context for the truth.

Present a positive view of what the Bible really says about the Trinity, Jesus Christ, mankind, and salvation. Show how the Biblical doctrines are more consistent, reasonable, and satisfying than the contradictory and inferior doctrines of The Way.

Express your love and respect for The Way follower you meet. Remember that it is false *teachings* we must guard against. We should love the *people* as ones for whom Christ died but who are deceived. For a Way follower to be willing to listen to the answer you have, he must be convinced that you have a genuine concern for him and that you are not attempting to deride him for his beliefs.

Finally, relate your life in Christ to him. Show him that your commitment to the Lordship of Jesus Christ, God the Son, fulfills you as The Way never could. Show him that he can find God's will and God's truth through his own study of the Bible, without Wierwille's props.

And don't be afraid to share your faith. Many people join The Way because they see people committed to a dynamic evangelism program. Show The Way member that he can share Christ and the truth of the gospel as zealously as he previously shared Wierwille's gospel.

When The Way member begins to see the problems in The Way, he needs someplace to go. He needs to know that there is something better—a secure relationship with the God of the Bible, in fellowship with other believers.

MARK MILLER

Mark Miller had forsaken everything for The Way. He was so convinced that it was God's organization for today that he had alienated himself from his friends, then his parents and in-laws, then his children, and finally his wife. None of them could see how God was working through The Way, and none would support him in his wholehearted involvement.

After five years of this, Mark's wife had finally left him and sued for divorce. She had refused to let their children attend meetings with him and had also refused to move the family to Ohio to be near The Way headquarters, where Mark had volunteered to run a portion of the mailing system. At the time, he said that he didn't care, that he was better off without his family if they couldn't submit to God's will. The only lonely times were on holidays or on the kids' birthdays. He had been given liberal visitation rights, but his work on the farm kept him so busy that he didn't often see them. But seeing them always depressed him.

Mark had attended his first Way Bible study at the invitation of a newcomer to his church, who had overheard Mark say that he was bored with the adult Sunday school class.

The newcomer, Albert, was Mark's age, in his mid-thirties, and seemed to radiate a love for other people and for God. Mark was infected by Albert's exuberant proclamation of the gospel to those he met even casually. He envied Albert's ability to witness unself-consciously. If only he could have God's power that way!

The Bible study turned out to be short that first night. Afterward Mark and the three other newcomers were told about an exciting self-help course that could teach them to share their faith and would revitalize their spiritual lives. The *Power for Abundant Living Course* had indeed revitalized Mark's life. It had so changed his perception of Christ and the Christian life that he actually began counting his salvation from that time onward instead of from the time he had gone forward at a Billy Graham crusade. Now he felt he knew why the charismatic movement was so dynamic. If only the other charismatics would join The Way!

UP AND OUT

Mark had always done things wholeheartedly. Whatever he got involved in, he immersed himself in. He immersed himself in The Way, and rose quickly within its ranks. Some of his superiors predicted that he would be one of the youngest leaders in the entire movement.

But another of Mark's personality traits was that he burned out quickly. After five years, shortly before his divorce, he began to tire of his 18-hour days and evening study times. The old thrill wasn't there anymore. There were no new challenges and no new excitements. He was invited to go fishing by the manager of the grocery store he frequented. They had talked several times when Mark had been shopping, and he liked Ted, the manager. Mark had a good time fishing with him, and it was only later that he realized it had been years since he had

had any social contacts outside of The Way. He thought he ought to feel a little guilty for having such a good time, but he didn't. It was like a breath of fresh air. He and Ted started fishing every Saturday morning, and they formed a solid friendship. They never discussed religion. Mark knew that Ted was a member of an evangelical church in town, and Ted knew that Mark was a Way member, but neither of them talked about it.

Six months after the fishing trips began, Mark first contemplated leaving the movement. He thought it would be nice to relax and just take things easy while he found something else exciting to join. Yes, he thought, it had come to that. His firm commitment to God's organization was fickle. His commitment was to excitement, not to truth, after all. He surprised everyone the day he turned in his resignation. He assured them that he had not talked to any deprogrammers, that he was not returning to his wife, and that he was not deep in sin. He was just tired of it all. He left no forwarding address and told no one but Ted where he was going.

During the next two years Mark kept up his support payments to his ex-wife but refused to let her know where he was living or what he was doing. He didn't come to see the children. Ted occasionally got postcards from him, but even he didn't know where Mark was. Ted had his Bible study and church pray weekly for Mark.

THE ROAD TO REALITY

Ted was surprised when he looked up one day to see Mark standing in front of him, smiling. Without explanation or greeting, Mark asked Ted if he could give him a job at the store to tide him over until he could find a job in his own field, computers. Ted hired him on the spot and then asked him where he had been and what he had been doing.

"That doesn't really matter, Ted. I've mostly just been bumming around, picking up odd jobs, talking to people, and relaxing. I guess you could say I've wasted the last two years as far as work is concerned. But I've been doing a lot of thinking. I've realized that I've never stuck with anything in my whole life. I've just had one temporary commitment after another. I don't really have anything permanent in my whole life. That's why I left The Way. I just got tired of it, like I get tired of everything. I think I need to change. Life isn't very satisfying this way. I'm going to start changing. But I don't know where to start. You seem so content and even happy with your life, Ted. Can you help me find the answers?"

Ted agreed, silently thanking God that he hadn't pushed Mark during the times they had fished, hoping that his own commitment to Christ and his happy life would prompt Mark to ask Ted about his Christian life and thereby give Ted the opportunity to show Mark the love and security of Christ in a natural way. He invited Mark home for dinner, and that night was the beginning of Mark's new life.

ALIVE AT LAST!

Mark's new life began with a sincere and complete surrender of his life to the Lordship of Jesus Christ, a surrender in prayer at Ted's home that first night. His growth as a Christian was slow and sometimes bumpy, and he had to resist his impulsiveness many times. But with the love and commitment of Ted, Ted's family, and the small church that Ted attended, Mark grew in faith and maturity.

Today, three years after he returned to Ted's store, Mark is a different man. He is still impulsive, and he still likes excitement, but he has a firm commitment to Christ and a sense of responsibility that he never had before. His children have spent the last two summers with him, and Mark and his ex-wife have discussed the desirability of his moving back to his hometown to be near the children. They have even discussed the distant possibility of getting back together. Mark realizes that The Way is not God's way, and he has even lectured at his home church about the unbiblical doctrines of The Way. He claims as his favorite Bible verse Philippians 1:6: "Being confident of this, that he who began a good work in you will carry it on to completion until the day of Christ Jesus."

8/ HELP FOR YOUR LOVED ONES IN A CULT

"Did she call?" Tom's drawn face reflected the worry in his voice as he came through the doorway, speaking to his wife who was hunched on the couch, eyes red and swollen from crying, fingers nervously shredding tissues. Tom kneeled by her, his arm reaching protectively around Dorothy's waist.

"Yes, she called, but it wasn't our Terri. She wasn't the same. She's changed. I don't even know her anymore. How could she do this to us? Where did we fail? Tom, it hurts too much, just too much. She said she only called so we wouldn't worry. She said she didn't love us anymore, that we had betrayed her by trying to talk her out of joining the Family of Love. She says she hates us, Tom. She actually told me she hated me!" Dorothy began crying quietly again.

"Did she tell you where she is? Did she tell you how we can get in touch with her? Did she say she would come visit? When is she coming home?" Urgency and fear were reflected in Tom's voice.

Through the tears Dorothy's voice, drained of emotion, intoned "Never, Tom, never. Our baby's never coming home. She said she wants to forget all about us. She wouldn't say where she is. She said we didn't matter anymore. She just wants to serve 'Father David.' I can't take it, Tom. I just can't believe it. I don't even want to live anymore. I hate myself. It's all my fault. I love her so much, but instead of telling her that, I just got mad and told her she was destroying us. It's so awful . . . I . . . I . . . I told her I wished she had died instead of hurting us like this. How could I have said it, Tom? I should be the one who died!"

The bitterness in his wife's voice increased Tom's confusion. He didn't know how to help Dorothy. He didn't know how to help Terri. He didn't even know how he felt himself. Why was he supposed to be the strong one in the family? Why couldn't he cry and rage like Dorothy? What could he do? It was no use. There was nothing to do. Tom dropped his arm from Dorothy's waist, rose slowly from the floor, and picked up his keys from the hall table. "I have to go out. I can't help you, Dorothy. I don't know what to do. I just have to get out of here. Maybe I'll go over to Pastor Green's house. Maybe he knows more about this than we do. I'm sorry, Dorothy."

Dorothy stared out the window without seeing. Her nervous fingers continued to fray the bits of tissue left in her hands. The only sound in the house was an intermittent sigh.

THERE IS A WAY

This story doesn't have to have a sad ending. It is possible to reach your loved ones in a cult. Even when we make mistakes, God can still leave a way for us to help our loved ones. In this conclusion to our survey of the cults at your doorstep, we will provide a workable plan for keeping your children from the cults and an effective plan for reaching your loved ones who are already in a cult. Finally, we'll tell you where you can go for further help for your loved ones.

KEEPING YOUR CHILDREN FROM THE CULTS

If your children never join a cult, you need never go through the agony expressed by Tom and Dorothy. Our Biblical goal as parents is to meet the emotional and spiritual needs of our children with the nourishment provided by the Word of God operating in our lives and in our families. Your child will never need to seek fulfillment in a cult if he has grown up fulfilled in Jesus Christ. Our experience has shown us that there are five important steps to producing children immune from the temptations of the world and the cults.

First, your family life must practice a cohesive and consistent Christian view of life. This means that your actions, individually and as a family, should always reflect your Christian commitment. Paul said in Philippians 1:9-11:

> And this is my prayer: that your love may abound more and more in knowledge and depth of insight, so that you may be able to discern what is best and may be pure and blameless until the day of Christ, filled with the fruit of righteousness that comes through Jesus Christ—to the glory and praise of God.

One of the favorite complaints against "Christendom" by the cults is that Christians are hypocrites—they teach one thing and do another. By maintaining a consistent Christian walk and openly facing the challenges of the world with the truth of God's Word, your family need never give your children occasion to see that cultic criticism leveled at himself, his parents, or his family.

Second, provide your children with a sound Bible background. A close familiarity with the whole Bible will prepare your children before their faith is challenged by the cults. By learning proper Bible study and interpretation at home, children are protected from the cults' replacement of

Bible study with warped cultic literature and unsound cultic interpretations of the Bible. Make Bible reading, study, and
discussion a regular part of your family routine.

Third, be sure that you are aware of your children's
emotional needs and that you are fulfilling those needs in ac-
cordance with God's will as revealed in the Bible. Children
need love, discipline, respect, comfort, joy, and all the other
nurturing emotional experiences that combine to develop an
adult with a healthy emotional outlook. Many people who join
the cults do so because they are promised the love and acceptance which they never found at home. Don't let your children starve emotionally so that even the poisonous diet of the
cults is appealing to them.

Fourth, don't neglect your children's spiritual needs.
Many people join cults because they have a genuine desire to
serve God and feel close to God, and those desires have been
frustrated at home and in their traditional churches. We
have a close friend (who now helps people get out of the cults)
who first joined a cult because he wanted to serve God but
didn't see anyone around him working zealously for God
except the people in the cult he soon joined. Provide your
children with the spiritual help they need and also provide
them with opportunities to be used by God in meeting other
people's spiritual needs. It is frustrating to want to do
something for God but then have everyone tell you that you
are not old enough or mature enough. We find that God often
uses our 2½-year-old daughter to minister to us spiritually
when we are spiritually weak! By allowing your children a
place of ministry within the family you are reinforcing their
self-worth and their relationship to God, and you are
strengthening your family's defenses against the world.

Fifth, commit your family to a local body of believers, a
church that actively practices the New Testament functions
of the body of Christ. One of the causes of the great cultic

growth in the 1970s, especially among young people, was the evangelical emphasis toward personal worship and away from ministry in the body of Christ. Christians need each other; God did not intend for us to live our Christian lives apart from our fellow believers. In Ephesians 4:11-16 Paul warns that those who are not grounded in the church are in danger of falling to false teachings:

It was he who gave some to be apostles, some to be prophets, some to be evangelists, and some to be pastors and teachers, to prepare God's people for works of service, so that the body of Christ may be built up until we all reach unity in the faith and in the knowledge of the Son of God and become mature, attaining to the whole measure of the fullness of Christ.

Then we will no longer be infants, tossed back and forth by the waves, and blown here and there by every wind of teaching and by the cunning and craftiness of men in their deceitful scheming. Instead, speaking the truth in love, we will in all things grow up into him who is the Head, that is, Christ. From him the whole body, joined and held together by every supporting ligament, grows and builds itself up in love, as each part does its work.

Your family needs the strong support of a church committed to the Biblical principles of supporting each other and evangelizing the world.

These five steps can go a long way in protecting your children from the cults.

BACK FROM THE CULTS

By now the pattern for successful evangelizing of cultists should be clear. Although the names and some of the heresies of the different cults may change, the members are all people just like you and I. But they have been deceived, and they desperately need to know the truth that is in Jesus Christ. There are various steps you can take in rescuing your loved one from a cult. We have listed below five of the most important steps.

First, and perhaps most important, love the cultist with the love of Christ. Love "is not rude, it is not self-seeking, it is not easily angered, it keeps no record of wrongs. Love does not delight in evil but rejoices with the truth. It always protects, always trusts, always hopes, always perseveres" (1 Corinthians 13:5-7). If you can communicate nothing else to the cultist, let him know that you love him without reservation or judgment, that you respect him as a sincere and honest human being who is trying to be happy and to serve God. This does not mean that you condone his beliefs or that you congratulate him for joining a cult! You can make it clear that while you disagree with what he has been taught, you love him as a person and want to see him happy and fulfilled.

Not long ago a Jehovah's Witness talked with us on the phone, and we invited him to stay with us (he lived almost 3000 miles away) when he came to our area to visit. He had many sincere questions, and we wanted him to feel that he had plenty of time to ask his questions and to get good, honest answers to them. He couldn't believe that we were willing to open our home to him, a Jehovah's Witness, when our occupation was to combat the teachings of the Watchtower. We spent hour after hour with him on the phone, and kept reassuring him of our love for him and our respect for his sincerity. Today, as a result of our continued work with him, and the work of other committed Christians, he has left the Watchtower and has committed his life to Jesus Christ. Less than three months old in the Lord, he is already learning to share his faith with others. He knows that the love of Christ works miracles!

Second, let your life be an example to your loved one of what a difference Christ can make. Your loved one who has joined a cult has probably been told that all of "Christendom" is hypocritical, and that he was lucky to get away from his family and its surface-level commitment to God's cause. If you maintain a consistent Christian life, your loved one won't be able to agree with what he is being taught. He will know that you have found fulfillment outside his cult but in the love of Jesus Christ. Let your life prove the cult wrong.

Third, in a loving and nonaggressive way, share with your loved one information on the cult and its heretical teachings. Don't shove anticult literature down his throat to choke him. Lovingly ask him if he would help you to understand his beliefs and how they relate to the Bible. Share with him your concern that he make his own decisions about what he is being taught. Express to him your confidence that he is capable of comparing his cult's teachings to the Bible to see if they measure up. There are many cultists who really don't know either the implications of what they have been taught or the true teachings of the Bible. Help get them on the road to a responsible personal choice concerning their beliefs.

Fourth, show your loved one that his emotional and spiritual needs (which probably drew him to the cult in the first place) can be met truly and permanently in a personal relationship with the Jesus of the Bible. He doesn't need an organization or leader mediating between him and God. "We have one who speaks to the Father in our defense—Jesus Christ, the Righteous One" (1 John 2:1).

Fifth, pray for your loved one in a cult. Your family should pray for him. You should be part of a church that is praying for him regularly and specifically. Prayer is powerful, and God uses our prayer as part of the orchestration of His plan. When someone calls us about his loved one in a cult, we make it a point to ask his first name and then pray for him specifically and regularly. Not only will prayer prove effective for your loved one, but it will also strengthen you, as David said: "When I called, you answered me; you made me bold and stouthearted"(Psalm 138:3).

In this book you have read the testimonies (with names and details changed) of people who have left the cults. It is possible for your loved one to leave the bondage of the cults and to enjoy freedom in Christ Jesus. Don't give up on him and don't give up on God's power. If you would like help from organizations designed to evangelize the cults, we have listed at the end of this chapter some groups that we know to be Christ-centered, effective, and responsible. Don't hesitate to call on any of us—that's what we're here for. We have also included our address and telephone number. If you need help with someone you love who is in a cult, or even if you have a question for which you need an answer, please call or write us. We care and we want to help.

DAVID AND JOANIE

We shared the gospel with a young Jehovah's Witness couple several years ago, using the principles that we shared in Chapter 3 and the format that we discussed in this chapter. They met with us at the insistence of their close friends, who had just become Christians and who were concerned for them. The Jehovah's Witness couple, David and Joanie Graham, came with their teachers from the Watchtower and at first refused to listen to us, saying that their teachers would do all the talking and listening. However, as we shared in love and prayed silently, David and Joanie began listening. When we expressed our concern for them and shared the life we had in Christ, they paid close attention. They seemed responsive when we contrasted the Christian life with life in the Watchtower. When we told them that they could go directly to God for forgiveness, love and guidance, without having to go through an organization or their teachers, they responded positively. When we assured them that they could read God's Word for themselves, all by itself, without any "aids" from the Watchtower, they agreed that this was Biblical.

The next morning Joanie called us. Her voice was happy and excited as it reflected the new freedom she had found. "I just had to call you today. I haven't talked to David since he went to work, and I don't know what he thinks about last night, but I know what I think. I prayed and searched the Bible like you said, and I know that the Watchtower is wrong and that Jesus is Jehovah and is my only Savior. I don't care what David does—I'm going to follow Jesus!"

Three hours later we received a call from David. "I'm on my lunch break and I don't have much time, but I need to see you both. I thought about what you said last night, and all morning I've been praying and trying to read my Bible when work slows down. The Jesus I heard about last night is the Jesus I met this morning in prayer! I know He's God and I know He'll forgive my sins freely. For the first time in my life I feel the love of God and I have the assurance of His Word that He loves me! When can I come over to talk some more?"

Joanie and David left the Watchtower that week. They later brought two of their friends out of the Watchtower, joined a good evangelical church, and began an active ministry to Jehovah's Witnesses. God was faithful and answered our prayers beyond what we had hoped!

Cultists do come to Christ, and it is possible to show your loved one in a cult your love for him and God's concern for his salvation. Jesus can reach your loved one and draw him to salvation and away from the bondage of the cults. Thousands of ex-cultists are testimony to the power of God working through His people in the body of Christ.

FOR FURTHER HELP

Robert and Gretchen Passantino
c/o CARIS (Christian Apologetics: Research and Information Service)
P.O. Box 2067
Costa Mesa, CA 92626
(714) 957-0249

CARIS Midwest Office
P.O. Box 1659
Milwaukee, WI 53201

Acts 17
P.O. Box 2183
La Mesa, CA 92041

CRI (Christian Research Institute)
P.O. Box 500
San Juan Capistrano, CA 92693

ICC (Institute for Contemporary Christianity)
P.O. Box A
Oakland, NJ 07436

New Directions Evangelistic Association
P.O. Box 2347
Burlington, NC 27215

PACE (Practical Apologetics and Christian Evangelism)
1944 No. Tustin Ave., Suite 118
Orange, CA 92665

Spiritual Counterfeits Project
P.O. Box 2418
Berkeley, CA 94702

RECOMMENDED READING

Adam, Ben. *Astrology: The Ancient Conspiracy*. Grand Rapids: Eerdmans, 1963.

Anderson, Einar. *The Inside Story of Mormonism*. Grand Rapids: Kregel. 1973.

Anderson, J.N.D. *Christianity and Comparative Religion*. Downers Grove: InterVarsity Press. 1970.

Anderson, Sir Norman, ed. *The World's Religions*. Downers Grove, IL: InterVarsity Press. 1976.

Boa, Kenneth. *Cults, World Religions, and You*. Wheaton: Victor, 1977.

Bjornstad, James. *Counterfeits at Your Door*. Glendale, CA: Gospel Light, 1979.

_____ . *Stars, Signs, and Salvation in the Age of Aquarius*. Grand Rapids: Bethany Fellowship, 1971.

Cowan, Marvin. *Mormon Claims Answered*. Salt Lake City: Marvin W. Cowan, n. d.

Cowdrey, Davis, and Scales with Passantino. *Who Really Wrote the Book Of Mormon?* Santa Ana, CA: Vision House, 1977.

Dencher, Ted. *Why I Left Jehovah's Witnesses*. Fort Washington, PA: Christian Literature Crusade, 1966.

Duddy, Neil, with SCP. *The God-Men*. Downers Grove, IL: InterVarsity Press, 1981.

Edwards, Christopher. *Crazy for God*. New York: Prentice-Hall, 1979.

Enroth, Ronald. *The Lure of the Cults*. Chappaqua, NY: Christian Herald, 1979.

_____ . *Youth, Brainwashing, and the Extremist Cults*. Grand Rapids: Zondervan, 1977.

Gardiner, Ron. *I Was a Jehovah's Witness*. Santa Ana, CA: CARIS, 1979.

Gruss, Edmund. *Apostles of Denial*. Nutley, NJ: Presbyterian and Reformed, 1970.

_____ . *Jehovah's Witnesses and Prophetic Speculation.* Nutley, NJ: Presbyterian and Reformed, 1972.

_____ . *We Left Jehovah's Witnesses, a Non-Prophet Organization*. Nutley, NJ: Presbyterian and Reformed, 1974.

Hefley, James. *The Youthnappers*. Wheaton: Victor, 1977.

Hoekema, Anthony. *Christian Science.* Grand Rapids: Eerdmans, 1963.

_____ . *Jehovah's Witnesses*. Grand Rapids: Eerdmans, 1963.

_____ . *Mormonism*. Grand Rapids: Eerdmans, 1963.

Hunt, Dave. *The Cult Explosion*. Eugene, OR: Harvest House, 1980.

Lewis, Gordon. *Confronting the Cults*. Grand Rapids: Baker, 1966.

_____ . *What Everyone Should Know About Transcendental Meditation*. Glendale, CA: Gospel Light, 1977.

Marsh, C. R. *Share Your Faith With a Muslim*. Chicago: Moody Press, 1975.

Martin, Walter. *The Maze of Mormonism*. Santa Ana, CA: Vision House, 1977.

_____ . *Kingdom of the Cults*. Grand Rapids: Bethany Fellowship, 1966.

_____ . ed., with Gretchen Passantino. *The New Cults*. Santa Ana, CA: Vision House, 1980.

_____ . *The Rise of the Cults*. Santa Ana, CA: Vision House, 1979.

Miller, Calvin. *Transcendental Hesitation*. Grand Rapids: Zondervan, 1977.

Miller, William M. *A Christian Response to Islam*. Nutley, NJ: Presbyterian and Reformed, 1976.

Montague, Havor. *Jehovah's Witnesses and Blood Transfusions*. Santa Ana, CA: CARIS, 1978.

Needleman, Jacob. *The New Religions*. New York: E. P. Dutton, 1976.

Parrinder, Jeffrey. *The Dictionary of Non-Christian Religions*. Philadelphia: Westminster Press, 1971.

Peterson, William J. *Those Curious New Cults*. New Cannaan, CN: Keats, 1975.

Rice, Mary Anne. *From Krishna to Christ*. Santa Ana, CA: CARIS, 1981.

Ridenour, Fritz. *So What's the Difference?* Glendale, CA: Gospel Light, 1967.

Sparks, Jack. *The Mind Benders*. Nashville, TN: Thomas Nelson, 1977, 1979.

Spittler, Russell. *Cults and Isms*. Grand Rapids: Baker, 1962.

Stoner and Parke. *All God's Children*. Radnor, PA: Chilton, 1977.

Tanner, Jerald and Sandra. *The Changing World of Mormonism*. Chicago: Moody, 1979.

Thomas, F.W. *Masters of Deception*. Grand Rapids: Baker, n. d.

Weldon, John, and Levitt, Zola. *The Transcendental Explosion*. Eugene, OR: Harvest House, 1976.

Van Buskirk, Michael. *The Scholastic Dishonesty of the Watchtower*. Santa Ana, CA: CARIS, 1977.

Williams, J.L. *Victor Paul Wierwille and the Way International*. Chicago: Moody, 1979.

Yamamoto, J. Isamu. *The Puppet Master*. Chicago: Moody, 1977.

Zaretsky, Irving and Leone. *Contemporary Religious Movements in America*. Princeton, NJ: Princeton University Press, 1974.

CHAPTER NOTES

Chapter 3
Answers to Jehovah's Witnesses

1. *Let God Be True* (New York: Watchtower Bible and Tract Society, Inc., 1946), p. 214.
2. Ibid., p. 213.
3. *The Watchtower*, Sept. 15, 1910, p. 288.
4. *Qualified to Be Ministers* (New York: WTBTS, 1955), p. 300.
5. Charles Taze Russell, *Studies in the Scriptures, The Time Is At Hand,* (New York: WTBTS, 1899), pp. 76-78.
6. *The Watchtower*, Sept. 1, 1916, p. 5950.
7. J. F. Rutherford, *Millions Now Living Will Never Die,* (New York: WTBTS, 1920), p. 97. (Now available in reprint from CARIS, P.O. Box 1783, Santa Ana, CA 92702.)
8. J. F. Rutherford, *Vindication* (New York: WTBTS, 1931), pp. 338-39.
9. For more coverage see Edmond Gruss, *Jehovah's Witnesses and Prophetic Speculation* (Nutley, NJ: Presbyterian and Reformed Publishers, 1972); and *Were You Told the Truth About 1975?* (Santa Ana, CA: CARIS).
10. *Let God Be True,* pp. 229, 231, 234.
11. *Blood, Medicine and the Law of God* (New York: WTBTS, 1961), p. 55.
12. Havor Montague, *Jehovah's Witnesses and Blood Transfusions* (Santa Ana, CA: CARIS, 1979), pp. 2, 3, 10, 12.
13. *The Truth That Leads to Eternal Life* (New York WTBTS, 1968), pp. 146, 148, 149.
14. *Is God Against Christmas?* reprinted from the Salvation Army *The Way Cry* (Santa Ana, CA: CARIS), p. 4.
15. *The Truth That Leads to Eternal Life, p. 14.*
16. *The Watchtower*, Sept. 15, 1910, p. 298.
17. *The Truth That Leads to Eternal Life, p. 25.*
18. It is best not to use the King James Version of 1 John 5:7 when talking with a Jehovah's Witness to try to prove the doctrine of the Trinity. There is serious doubt as to its appearance in the original manuscripts of the New Testament, and the Witness has been taught to discount it because of its supposed spurious origin.
19. *Let God Be True,* p. 89.
20. *The Kingdom Is At Hand* (New York: WTBTS: 1944), pp. 46, 47, 49.
21. Other verses showing that Jesus is God: Titus 2:13; John 8:58; Romans 9:5.
22. *Let God Be True,* p. 185.
23. Ibid., p. 272.
24. *The Truth that Leads to Eternal Life,* p. 25.
25. Ibid., pp. 34-35.
26. Julius R. Mantey, *Is Death the Only Punishment for Unbelievers?* (Santa Ana, CA: CARIS).
27. *Aid to Bible Understanding* (New York: WTBTS, 1971), p. 1373.
28. Ibid., p. 1443.

Chapter 4
Answers to the Mormons

1. Jeffrey Kay, *"An Invisible Empire: Mormon Money in California,"* in *New West Magazine,* May 8, 1978, pp. 36-40.
2. Ezra Taft Benson, *Fourteen Fundamentals in Following the Prophets.* Speech transcript of the Brigham Young University Devotional Assembly, Tuesday, Feb. 26, 1980, 10:00 A.M.
3. Joseph Smith, Jr., "The History of Joseph Smith the Prophet," in *The Pearl of Great Price* 2:18,19.
4. For a thorough discussion of Mormonism, and racism, see Walter Martin's *The Maze of Mormonism,* Chapter 5, "Mormonism's Racism," pp. 151-94.
5. For a thorough discussion of the origin of *The Book of Mormon,* see *Who Really Wrote the Book of Mormon?* by Howard Davis, Donald Scales, and Wayne Cowdrey with Gretchen Passantino.
6. Daniel Hendriz, personal testimony, property of the Chicago Historical Society.
7. Jerald and Sandra Tanner, *Mormonism: Shadow or Reality* (Salt Lake City: Modern Microfilm Co., 1971), pp. 14-31.
8. For further reading on Bible reliability, see the Recommended Reading list on page 195 of this book.
9. *Doctrine and Covenants* 130:22.
10. Joseph Smith, Jr., *History of the Church* 6:484.
11. See also the following verses. For *the Father* see 1 Timothy 2:5; 2 Peter 1:17; Matthew 5:45; 11:25; John 5:18; 2 Corinthians 1:3. For *the Son* see Titus 2:13; John 1:1; 5:18; 8:58; 20:28; Revelation 1:17 (c.f. Isaiah 41:4); Revelation 22:12,13 (cf. 1:8; 21:6); 1 Corinthians 2:8 (cf. Psalm 24:8-10); Isaiah 9:6; Hebrews 1:8; Romans 9:5. For *the Holy Spirit* see Hebrews 9:14; Psalm 139:7-10; Job 33:4; Acts 28:25-27 (cf. Isaiah 6:8-10); Acts 5;3,4.
12. Brigham Young, *Journal of Discourses* 1:50,51.
13. There are competent Christian experts who have capably covered the Mormon doctrine of Adam-God before us. Notable among them is Chris Vlachos, who reported his findings in the *Journal of Pastoral Practice,* Vol. III, No. 2, pp. 93-119, "Brigham Young's False Teaching: Adam is God." We feel that discussions of this type are not advised for the average Christian witnessing to the average Mormon. Since Mormonism now denies the teaching, it seems futile to first convince the Mormon at your door that his prophet taught it, then that the Mormons should believe their prophet, and then that the teaching is false. For the average encounter, it is better to avoid this subject altogether.
14. Joseph Fielding Smtih, *Doctrines of Salvation,* compiled by McConkie, Vols. I-III (Salt Lake City: Bookcraft, 1955).

Chapter 5
Answers to the Moonies

1. *Chicago Sun-Times,* Aug. 28, 1980.
2. Orange County *Register* (Santa Ana, CA), March 16, 1977, p. A16.
3. *A.D.* magazine, May 1974, p. 33.
4. *Time* magazine, Sept. 30, 1974, p. 69.

5. *Divine Principle*, 2nd ed. (The Holy Spirit Association for the Unification of World Christianity, 1973), p. 9.
6. See, for example, W. Arndt, *Does the Bible Contradict Itself?* (St. Louis, Concordia, n.d.); Donald Guthrie, *New Testament Introduction* (Downers Grove, IL: InterVarsity Press, 1965); John Haley, *Alleged Discrepancies in the Bible* (Nashville: Gospel Advocate, n.d.); R. K. Harrison, *Introduction to the Old Testament* (Grand Rapids: Eerdmans, 1969); Harold Lindsell, *The Battle for the Bible* (Grand Rapids: Zondervan, 1976); J.A.T. Robinson, *Can We Trust the New Testament?* (Grand Rapids: Eerdmans, 1977).
7. See, for example, Norman Geisler and William Nix, *From God to Us* (Chicago: Moody Press, 1974); R. Laird Harris, *Inspiration and Canonicity of the Bible* (Grand Rapids: Eerdmans, 1969); Rene Pache, *The Inspiration and Authority of Scripture* (Chicago: Moody Press, 1969); Merrill C. Tenney, *The Bible: The Living Word of Revelation* (Grand Rapids: Zondervan, 1968).
8. *Divine Principle,* p. 212.
9. *The Master Speaks-7* (HSAUWC, transcribed messages from 1965), p. 4.
10. *Divine Principle,* p. 151.
11. Ibid., p. 215.
12. Ibid., pp. 147-148.

Chapter 6
Answers to the Hare Krishnas

1. Transcript from *Prime Time Sunday,* NBC Television, July 1, 1979, 10 P.M. broadcast, Tom Snyder, host.
2. *Srimad Bhagavatam* 1:3:28 (Bhaktivendanta).
3. *Jesus Loves Krsna* (Los Angeles Bhaktivendanta), p. 26.
4. Ibid., p. 37.
5. Ibid., p. 52.
6. Jananibas das Brahmacari, "KRSNA-consciousness Is the Absolute Necessity for Mankind in This Age," in *Back to Godhead,* No. 34, p. 24.
7. Abhay Charan De Bhaktivendanta Swami Prabhupada, *Bhagavad-Gita As It Is* (Bhaktivendanta), 4:30.
9. Ibid., p. 326.

Chapter 7
Answers to The Way International

1. "The Way Seemed Right But the End Thereof . . . ", in *Eternity,* Nov. 1977, pp. 23-35.
2. *National Courier Magazine,* April 1, 1977, p. 4.
3. *Twenty-fifth Anniversary Souvenir Booklet* (New Knoxville, OH: The Way, Inc., 1967), p. 12.
4. Elena Whiteside, *The Way: Living in Love* (New Knoxville, OH: American Christian Press, 1970), p. 175.
5. *This Is The Way* (New Knoxville, OH: The Way, Inc., n.d.), side one.
6. Ibid.
7. *Twenty-fifth Anniversay Souvenir Booklet,* p. 17.
8. Victor Paul Wierwille, *Power for Abundant Living* (New Knoxville, OH: American Christian Press, 1971), pp. 207-11.

9. Walter Martin, ed., *The New Cults* (Santa Ana, CA: Vision House Publishers, 1980), p. 47.
10. Victor Paul Wierwille, *Jesus Christ Is Not God* (New Knoxville, OH: American Christian Press, 1975), p. 5.
11. Ibid., p. 16.
12. Ibid., p. 82.
13. A. T. Robertson, *Word Pictures in the New Testament,* Vol. 5 (Nashville, TN: Broadman Press, 1932), p. 3.
14. Victor Paul Wierwille, *Receiving the Holy Spirit Today* (New Knoxville, OH: American Christian Press, n.d.), pp. 3-5.
15. *Power for Abundant Living,* pp. 258-59.
16. Victor Paul Wierwille, *Are the Dead Alive Now?* (Old Greenwich, CN: Devin-Adair Co., n.d.), p. 97.
17. *Receiving the Holy Spirit Today,* p. 148.
18. *Power for Abundant Living,* p. 313.
19. *Eternity* magazine, p. 6.

SCRIPTURE INDEX

ABOUT THE AUTHORS

Cult experts Robert and Gretchen Passantino are well-known for their research, lectures, and writing in the field of religious cults and sects. Robert Passantino is the Director of Christian Apologetics: Research and Information Service. Gretchen Passantino is a contributing author to the authoritative work *The New Cults* (Walter Martin, General Editor) and is a coauthor of *Who Really Wrote the Book of Mormon?* Raymond Schafer has had wide experience in editing and writing, and his co-authored books appeal to a wide variety of readers who want authoritative answers presented in concise and readable form.